Leaders on Leadership

Thank you for choosing a SAGE product! If you have any comment, observation or feedback, I would like to personally hear from you. Please write to me at contactceo@sagepub.in

—Vivek Mehra, Managing Director and CEO,
SAGE Publications India Pvt Ltd, New Delhi

Bulk Sales

SAGE India offers special discounts for purchase of books in bulk. We also make available special imprints and excerpts from our books on demand.

For orders and enquiries, write to us at

Marketing Department
SAGE Publications India Pvt Ltd
B1/I-1, Mohan Cooperative Industrial Area
Mathura Road, Post Bag 7
New Delhi 110044, India
E-mail us at marketing@sagepub.in

Get to know more about SAGE, be invited to SAGE events, get on our mailing list. Write today to marketing@sagepub.in

This book is also available as an e-book.

Leaders on Leadership

Insights from Corporate India

All India Management Association

www.sagepublications.com

Los Angeles • London • New Delhi • Singapore • Washington DC

First published in 2012 by

SAGE Response
B1/I-1 Mohan Cooperative Industrial Area
Mathura Road, New Delhi 110 044, India

SAGE Publications Inc
2455 Teller Road
Thousand Oaks, California 91320, USA

SAGE Publications Ltd
1 Oliver's Yard, 55 City Road
London EC1Y 1SP, United Kingdom

SAGE Publications Asia-Pacific Pte Ltd
33 Pekin Street
#02-01 Far East Square
Singapore 048763

Management House
14, Institutional Area
Lodhi Road,
New Delhi 110 003
India

Published by Vivek Mehra for SAGE Publications India Pvt Ltd, typeset in 11/17 Berkeley Oldstyle Book by Diligent Typesetter, Delhi and printed at Saurabh Printers Pvt. Ltd.

Library of Congress Cataloging-in-Publication Data

Leaders on leadership/edited by All India Management Association
        p. cm.
     1. Leadership—India—Case studies. 2. Executives—India—Case studies.
3. Leadership—Case studies. I. All India Management Association.
HD57.7.L425   658.4'092—dc23   2012   2012033102

ISBN: 978-81-321-1049-1 (PB)

The SAGE Team: Sachin Sharma, Shreya Chakraborti, Nand Kumar Jha and Dally Verghese

Contents

Foreword

During my long association with All India Management Association (AIMA), I have wondered about how to better transmit the lessons learnt by successful Indian leaders to upcoming managers. An entire generation of our managers is facing serious and persistent adversity in crafting the future. They are struggling to cope and are hoping for the return of the easy times. In reality, this is also a call to assume leadership and help their organizations to adapt. This book might instruct and inspire them.

The authors in this book are all winners of prestigious awards instituted by AIMA, including the Managing India Awards, JRD Tata Corporate Leadership Award, AIMA Life Time Achievement Award, etc., for their inspiring transformational leadership. These are all outstanding individuals who have achieved great success despite odds. They are widely regarded as role models for upcoming managers. These are business leaders who blossomed during a past period of great change—domestic liberalization and global integration of Indian economy. Those in family businesses had to transform their groups to adapt to the new world and the professionals, and the entrepreneurs had to align themselves to the new opportunities.

Traditionally, leadership has been considered to be either an inheritance for those born in powerful families or a born trait among some who went on to acquire power. However, through the past century, as management became a knowledge discipline, there have been significant changes in the way people think about leadership.

Increasingly, leadership is being looked at more as a competence and less as a trait. While individual characteristics—intelligence, courage, charm, etc.—remain relevant to leadership, the situational and organizational factors now play a greater role in performing the leadership function.

Much like Darwin's theory of survival of the fittest, no individual can successfully lead in all situations and circumstances, howsoever naturally gifted. So, different times throw different kinds of leaders. It is about suitability and adaptability, and not a personality ideal.

Leadership remains a challenge for most people. But, for the ambitious, there is no option but to learn leadership. Most young people find too much hype in the magazine and the media to actually imbibe anything useful from them. This book overcomes that problem.

It is a compilation of self-narrated leadership experiences of India's business leaders. The variety of their backgrounds, challenges, and achievements makes this book even more enriching. Beyond the generic basics, leadership remains a very personal quest and achievement linked to one's unique personality, circumstances, and challenges.

I feel that this book will equip the reader to face the task of leadership with much greater confidence and clarity. It is my sincere hope that the book will significantly improve our leadership stock, which is needed to put India into the next orbit of economic growth and global competitiveness.

R. Gopalakrishnan
Director, Tata Sons,
Mumbai

Preface

Much of the leadership literature in the business education domain is too formal, too didactic. Leadership, however, has too significant a personal element to be left to a generic design. This book is born out of that need for learning from example.

AIMA has been organizing conferences and conversations on leadership. It facilitates dialogue among business leaders and between iconic business leaders and young managers. While these events have benefited those who could participate, AIMA realized the need to put out literature on leadership that is instructive in an engaging and friendly manner.

The book is meant to serve both as a set of case studies for management students and as an insightful account of contemporary Indian business leadership. It is as much a reference book as it is a piece of serious business literature.

This book was conceived as a set of lessons in leadership in contemporary India in the voice of the leaders themselves. It was structured around personal experiences, challenges, and achievements. So, instead of being another theoretical exercise in understanding the nature and tools of leadership, this book is an account of leadership experience in the real world.

This book is structured as a compilation of short personal narratives by iconic business leaders of their leadership beliefs and experiences. One of the key findings of the books is that even the most accomplished leaders had to discover their leadership calling and develop their leadership traits with conscious initiative and practice. The book allows the reader to appreciate the journey of the authors from regular individuals to iconic leaders and draw inspiration from their struggles and achievements.

One of the key challenges of putting such a book together was the selection of the authors. During the past couple of decades, India has witnessed the emergence of several globally acknowledged business leaders. Many of them are inheritors who transformed traditional business empires, and many others are first generation entrepreneurs who utilized the opportunities thrown up by economic liberalization and globalization to build business empires in their own lifetime.

AIMA decided to draw on the pool of its management award winners to write the different chapters of this book. As the apex body of management occupation in the country, AIMA has been the touchstone for recognition of business leadership for 56 years. Every year, AIMA presents some of the most coveted management awards in the country. These include the AIMA-JRD Tata Corporate Leadership Award, AIMA Lifetime Achievement Award,

AIMA Public Service Excellence Award, and AIMA Managing India Awards for Transformational Business Leadership, Emerging Business Leaders of the Year, Outstanding Institution Builder, Corporate Citizen of the Year, and Outstanding PSU of the Year. To make the book contemporary, AIMA decided to stick with the more recent winners of its major awards. AIMA shortlisted the most iconic of the present generation of business leaders and requested them to provide their personal prescriptions for learning to lead, illustrated with their own experience in learning and practicing leadership. Some of them chose to write themselves while some others were interviewed by AIMA for their personal stories.

The authors have provided rare biographical details and shared their self-scrutiny in these chapters. They have offered insights into the challenges they faced at important junctures of their careers and at the times of change in their business. They have got candid about their fears and hopes and their personal ways to deal with those. The reader would get the feeling that they know the person behind the celebrity.

AIMA is grateful to all the remarkable authors who have provided outstandingly lucid narratives that make this book a wonderful read. Mr N. R. Narayana Murthy, Founder, Infosys; Mr Deepak Parekh, Chairman, HDFC; Mr Kumar Managalam Birla, Chairman, Aditya Birla Group; Mr Adi Godrej, Chairman, Godrej Group; Ms Chanda Kochar, Managing Director and Chief Executive Officer, ICICI Bank; Mr Raghav Bahl, Managing Director, Network 18; Mr M. V. Subbiah, former Chairman, Murugappa Group;

Mr Tarun Das, former Director General, CII, have opened up to the reader like never before. AIMA is indebted to them for allowing the concept of a unique leadership instruction to take the shape of this book.

This book is a result of a lot of coordinated hard work of nearly a year. Some editing had to be done to achieve simplicity and brevity in the chapters. Sincere effort has been made to preserve the accuracy and substance of the original contributions.

AIMA is also grateful to SAGE Publications India for publishing the book. Thanks to SAGE, the book is nicely produced and is made widely available to the readers.

Chapter 1

Lessons from the Infosys Journey

—N. R. Narayana Murthy

Infosys was founded in 1981 by seven software professionals from different backgrounds with complementary skills, a
similar value system, a modest capital of US$250, and a pow-
erful idea. The idea was to specialize in developing large, custom-
ized quality software applications for global customers, leveraging
the Global Delivery Model (GDM). We split the software development task to two groups. The first set of tasks were undertaken
out of the client's office and the second set of tasks that had lower
interaction levels with the client were delivered out of talent-rich,
process-driven, scalable, and cost-competitive development centers in countries like India. This model was further enhanced by the
24-hour productive day created by combining the time difference

1

between the US and India, allowing us to deliver quality software on time and within budgeted cost to our customers.

Forming Infosys

During the 1980s, the business environment in India was not conducive for entrepreneurship. The landscape was dominated by a handful of family-owned conglomerates. Byzantine government regulations and import restrictions made it extremely difficult for any new business to start or succeed. In the backdrop of these challenging times, Infosys was started from humble beginnings. We were strong on hard work, commitment, energy, enthusiasm, and confidence. By overcoming challenges, we remained focused on building the company. As of March 31, 2012, Infosys had annual revenues of US$6.99 billion and net income of US$1.72 billion. Infosys has been voted the most respected, the best employer, the best managed, and the best in corporate governance in India.

Over the past three decades of this journey, I have learnt several lessons. One of the important lessons has been of leadership and its role in the success of a company. Before I share my lessons on leadership, let me share my perspectives on who is a leader and what is leadership.

Who Is a Leader? What Is Leadership?

The primary task of a leader is to be a change agent whose core responsibility is to raise the aspirations of the people. The leader has to make them more confident, energetic, enthusiastic, hopeful, and determined to seek a glorious future for the company, community, and for themselves.

Many a times, leaders have to walk the untrodden path, the road less traveled, and have to take huge risks. Robert Kennedy summed up the leadership challenge best when, borrowing the words of George Bernard Shaw, he said, "Most people see things as they are and wonder why; I dream of things that never were and say, 'why not?'"[1] To me, this is perhaps the best description of the leadership challenge. The challenge is to see what most people do not see, to accept what most people wonder about and are scared of, and then say, "I will take up this challenge because it is aspirational, honorable, and it is the right thing to do."

Building Infosys, to the company it is today, was a constant endeavor to make the impossible look possible. It was about raising the aspirations of our employees, making them dream big, and enabling them to achieve those aspirations. In 1981, when we were just seven people starting Infosys, we set out to become the most-respected global corporation. It seemed audacious then but it was made possible by our aspirations and action.

By founding Infosys, heading it as the CEO for the first 21 years and as the chairman of the board for the first 25 years, I have learnt many lessons on leadership.

---

[1] Robert Kennedy recited this version of what Shaw wrote in *Back to Methuselah* (1947, Oxford University Press) so often that many sources credit the words to him with no mention of Shaw. Kennedy himself usually noted that he was quoting Shaw in his speeches, although his version was actually a paraphrase of Shaw, rather than an exact quote.

Articulate a Powerful Vision

What is the first and foremost task of a leader? It is creating a grand vision and a purpose which is noble, lofty, and aspirational. It is a dream that should excite and energize everybody in the community or a corporation. The leader has to craft and articulate a vision in which everyone sees a better future for himself or herself. The vision has to be powerful enough to make every tired mind and body that leaves the office in the evening to return the next day saying, "I am proud to belong to this company, and I will work hard to make it a better company."

When the seven of us met in the small room in my apartment in Bombay in May 1981, we had a four-hour long discussion to define the vision for the company. After many deliberations on whether we should be the largest software services company, largest job creators, or have the highest market capitalization, I suggested,

> We should be the most-respected software services company in the world. If you seek respect, you will not shortchange your customers, you will be fair to your colleagues in the company, you will be transparent with your investors, you will treat your vendor partners with care and understanding, you will not violate the laws of the land in whatever country you operate, and you will live in harmony in whatever society you operate in. My conviction is that such a pursuit will bring revenues, jobs, profits, and market capitalization.

My fellow founders concurred with this vision. They perceived this vision for Infosys as something that was larger than life. They found it more inspirational than merely chasing profits, revenues, and market capitalization. Over the years, we have worked steadfastly to fulfill this vision. As a result, our revenues and profits have grown, jobs have been created, and market capitalization has increased.

COMMUNICATE VISION AND VALUES

After defining a powerful and attractive vision, a leader has to communicate that vision to a large number of people in the organization. It is very unlikely that leaders will be able to talk to everyone of their employees. To overcome this challenge, a leader should create mechanisms and processes through which the vision and values of the company can be constantly communicated and reinforced.

For example, today, Infosys is a company with 150,000 people. We operate in 33 countries and have employees from 88 nationalities. No matter how hard we try, it is not possible for us to interact one-on-one with every one of our employees. Hence, we use several indirect and surrogate mechanisms to communicate our vision to a large group of people in the company—simple and powerful quotes, multiple tiers of leaders, meeting in small groups and, most importantly, leadership-by-example.

Communication is most impactful and yields best results when it is simple, and direct. Ideas should be conveyed through powerful statements or quotes. At Infosys, our vision is *to be a globally respected corporation.* This is a good vision but would have failed unless we brought exhilaration, joy, enthusiasm, and energy to the minds of our people to translate this vision to reality. Hence, we use the famous adage, "A plausible impossibility is better than a convincing possibility," to make every Infoscion remember that their mission is to satisfy our customers by making the plausibly impossible happen. We want them to reach for the impossible in every situation because it is plausible, it is inspirational, and it is desirable rather than reach for the mundane and easily attainable goals in satisfying the customer.

Similarly, we use other quotes to facilitate easy and direct communication of our values, duties, obligations, beliefs, dreams, and aspirations. For example, our value system is communicated by the simple adage, "The softest pillow is a clear conscience." Our commitment to transparency is communicated by the adage, "When in doubt, disclose."

Demonstrate Commitment to Values

A value system is the protocol for behavior of an individual in a group, which is required to enhance the trust, confidence, energy, enthusiasm, and hope of every other individual in the group. Value system is extremely essential as working towards an aspirational objective involves team work and sacrifice from every member of the corporation. The leader should lead the way by demonstrating commitment to values on a regular basis so as to not make the value system a pure rhetoric.

Let me share an example. In 1995, we had to wait for a few months for permission from the Government of India to start an office in Boston. So, we decided to invest the money, ear-marked for setting up the new office, in the secondary market and get some returns in the interim. It turned out that we did not have enough expertise to invest successfully in the second-ary market, and we made some losses. At that time, according to the Indian General Accepted Accounting Principle (GAAP), it was not mandatory to provide the details of the losses in non core business activities. Since we had made a commitment to our shareholders that we would bring them the bad news early and pro-actively, I said, "I want be known to our shareholders as an honest person first, and then a smart person. So, let us give them full details of our losses." We communicated the loss to our shareholders with the assurance that we will learn from our mistakes. While many of my friends in the Indian corporate world were surprised by this move, shareholders were happy about our transparency.

Today, Infosys has many recognition schemes in the company to honor employees who imbibe and practice Infosys values. We honor those individuals who have demonstrated Infosys values best in their day-to-day action as Value champions.

Build Trust

Every aspirational objective requires tremendous courage, hard work, team work, and sacrifice. How do leaders ensure that their people commit to such hard work and sacrifice in the hope of a better future? To get such commitment from employees, a leader has to become trustworthy.

When a leader articulates a vision to a group or a function, it is generally seen as pure rhetoric or, at best, a statement of lofty purpose. There is no data to prove that the aspirational objective will be met. There is an element of risk, as a leader leads the team on a road less traveled or, sometimes, even on a road not traveled at all. To overcome this fear, a leader has to create and nurture a bond of trust with the employees for them to follow.

At Infosys, we have looked at various instruments to create trust. After considerable thinking and researching, we realized that the best instrument for creating trust is to demonstrate our commitment to our vision and values through leadership-by-example or "walking-the-talk." More than anything else, this will help leaders in earning the trust and commitment of their people.

Demonstrate Courage

I was once asked by the CEO of a Fortune 10 corporation the first attribute that a leader must have if his other attributes must find utterance. It took me 10 seconds to say "courage." He asked me, "Why do you think courage is the most important attribute of a leader?" I said,

> If you want to walk the untrodden path, if you want to dream big, if you want the organization to take risks, if you want to have conviction, if you want to go against the conventional wisdom, if you want to take tough and unpopular decisions, if you want to communicate to your people that a plausible impossibility is better than a convincing possibility, then you must have courage.

He seemed quite satisfied!

I do not know of any great leader, whether in a corporation or a nation, who did not demonstrate courage. This is a key attribute that is at the heart of leadership. Without courage other attributes will not find utterance.

In 1994, one of our large clients, who contributed a quarter of Infosys revenues, was looking to renegotiate billing rates. We had an internal discussion and came to the conclusion that reducing rates would probably dilute our commitment to that customer and let them down in front of their customers. Therefore, we decided to hold to our stance and refused to sign the contract at a lower rate. While this resulted in short pain from the loss of a large client, we gained in our determination to be open and honest with our customers.

Be Open and Fair

I believe that being open and fair is another powerful way by which leaders can earn the trust of their people. In the Indian culture, family is a very strong unit and brings the best of sacrifice, kindness, openness, and fairness from the members. So, I often tell my colleagues, "When you deal with your colleagues, you have to operate as if you are in a family." So, at Infosys, all doors are open at all points of time. Any employee is welcome to walk into the office of anyone to discuss issues. The best way of ensuring fairness in a transaction is to use data and facts to decide on the merits of the transaction. By doing so, the confidence of the employees is boosted by the fairness and openness in the system. Even those who lose a transaction are likely to say, "My boss tried hard to be fair to me. Next time, if I have better data and facts on my side, I will win." This way, people are confident to work smarter and harder even after they lose a transaction. Our commitment to openness and fairness is exemplified by the famous adage, "In God we trust, everybody else brings data to the table!" It is the duty of a good leader to create open and fair systems in the organization to create a trusting environment.

Create an Inclusive Environment

Another important leadership lesson I have learnt in motivating people is the power of inclusion. Self-esteem is a great motivator for human beings. Self-esteem gets enhanced when people participate in making decisions that affect them. In other words, a leader cannot create two classes of people—those that rule and those that are ruled. An inclusive system enhances the self-esteem, enthusiasm, energy, confidence, and hope of everyone in the organization. Such a system helps people deal with their fellow colleagues with respect, dignity, and affection. A good leader will spend time and energy in creating such an inclusive system to create a collective harmony.

Practice Good Corporate Governance

Practicing good corporate governance is the first duty of a good leader. Corporate governance is the governance mechanism used in a company to maximize shareholder value, on a sustainable basis, while ensuring fairness, transparency, and accountability with every stakeholder—customers, employees, investors, vendor-partners, government-of-the-land, and the society. At Infosys, we adhere to the best global practices of corporate governance. In fact, Infosys adopted the stringent US GAAP many years before other companies in India did.

Lay Down a Clear Operating Philosophy

As the embodiment of corporate leadership, a CEO has additional responsibility for ensuring the sustainability of the corporation. I define a CEO's job as ensuring PSPD—ensuring predictability of revenues by a good forecasting system that derives data from the trenches; sustaining those predictions by ensuring sales, producing, and delivering quality products and services on time, raising invoices and collecting money on time; ensuring good profits, achieved legally and ethically; and finally, ensuring that the business is de-risked through systems and processes that ensure minimization of risk to the corporation in every dimension of its operation.

A Leader Is Nothing Without People to Lead

A final lesson that I have learnt is that "leadership is not about oneself." It is about raising aspirations and creating confidence, joy, hope, enthusiasm, and energy of others. To do this, a leader must behave in a manner that will make people flock to seek help, solace, guidance, confidence, and joy. Good leaders are generous, confident, decisive, firm yet courteous, and make people feel an inch taller in their presence. Good leaders are also not afraid to show their frailties, share their emotions, and dissipate any thoughts of superiority among their people. Above all, a leader should be humble. They should act according to the adage, "Take your work seriously but do not take yourself too seriously."

By imbibing all of these attributes, a leader can become a role model worthy of emulation by people.

Chapter 2

Carrying on the Leadership Tradition

—M. V. Subbiah

What is leadership? I am not sure I know the answer to that question, in spite of the quantum of sociological debate on the subject, and in spite of specific attributes being identified as being essential to being a "leader." Whatever I have done or achieved has been intuitive, based on things that have been important organizationally as well as individually (for me) at specific points in time as well as over time.

Let me start this narrative with a couple of disclaimers. One, I was a bad student through school and college; in fact, I did not complete my graduation. Two, most of what has been credited to me as my achievements have been the result of the ground-work done by my earlier generations—I essentially carried on the tradition.

When you read this chapter, you might get a sense of a strong running thread of continuity and design in what I did. Be aware that that is a function of retrospect—when one looks back, one is able to identify and label some running themes which may not have been evident at the actual time of action. If anything, however, it might be indicative of my cultural moorings, which have guided me through life—professional as well as personal.

Family and tradition have been two of the most important underpinnings of what I did, and the rest essentially came out of these. Over the years, the institution of family has nurtured in me great values, provided me with the space to hone my skills, and given me the vital understanding that the combined efforts of people will always be greater than individual skill. It is often said that five fingers are not alike, but that it takes all of them together to grasp—accomplish—things. My family recognized this early. I remember the day my uncle summoned me, handed me a wooden pencil, and asked me to break it. I took it and snapped it easily. He then gave me a bunch of six pencils (six because we were six cousins in my generation) and asked me to similarly break them. I couldn't.

Family for me meant the entire gamut of a joint family, though I lost my father when I was seven years old. There was no difference between siblings and cousins. We ate together, went to school together, and went on holidays together. All occasions—from the breakfast table, family lunches to Sunday get-togethers—included members of every generation and, as such, were an investment in the future, with an atmosphere of trust and mutual respect.

Now a bit of history to anchor my story and my life. The Murugappa group was started by a visionary man—my grandfather Dewan Bahadur—who had a vision of building his own empire and, at the same time, strengthening the institution of the family. He went to Burma (now Myanmar) in 1898 at the age of 14 years to work as a banking clerk for another Chettiar family business. In those days, the British ruled India, Burma, Malaysia, and Ceylon (now Sri Lanka). A bright man, he started his own banking and trading business a few years later—first opening a branch in Burma, followed by Malaysia and Ceylon. Each branch was looked after by an agent who held a 25 percent share in the local business—what we today call stock options. Within two decades, Dewan Bahadur had built a financial institution that was the largest private bank in lower Burma.

Over the decades, the family enterprise grew through a variety of forms: start-ups, acquisitions, joint ventures, diversification, vertical integration, public offerings, and divestitures—different growth strategies addressing the evolving political and economic situation. Up to 1987, each business unit was run by a hands-on family owner/manager, and most decisions were made at the individual company level. With the opening up of the Indian economy, and in the interests of competitiveness, we became a "group" in a more formal way and officially constituted the Murugappa Corporate Board (MCB); the group corporate committee was set up in 1987 and the MCB in 1990. The new competitive environment required speedier and more flexible group business portfolio decisions, and the MCB was set up with the aim of exchanging ideas, advice, and knowledge—a practice that had decreased over the years as the businesses grew larger and more diverse and the families farther from one another than in the past. (I shall go into the details of this transition later in this chapter.)

Today, headquartered in Chennai, the ₹170,510 million Murugappa group is active in diverse areas of business including engineering, abrasives, finance, general insurance, cycles, sugar, farm inputs, fertilizers, plantations, bio-products, and nutraceuticals. Its 29 companies have manufacturing facilities spread across 13 states in India and have a combined workforce of over 32,000 employees.

So, it was in such a collegial environment that I grew up and started work. My grandfather and then my eldest uncle trained successors in an interesting way for that time. We were all sent to agents for training and apprenticeship—I was the last one to be trained his way. During 1952–1953 and 1953–1954, my last two years at high school, I was sent for summer vacations to Sri Lanka to train with an agent there. The routine was to start from the bottom and, if competence allowed, slowly work upwards. My first day as a *podian*—a peon—was traumatic; I was ordered by the agent to go and buy a *paan* for him. Ordinarily, it shouldn't have been a difficult task but for the fact that I didn't know, in a totally new place, where to buy it! However, the entire experience was unforgettable and instructive, not only for the novelty of the situation but also because it taught me humility, dignity of labor and, of course, discipline. Discipline was crucial—in my second year of apprenticeship, if I didn't tally the cash book every evening and put the cash box into the safe, I was not to have dinner!

These values got reinforced in another formative experience. During an unsuccessful attempt at earning an engineering degree at Birmingham, my mentor–professor saw the writing on the wall and told me that I should give up any thoughts of engineering. Instead, he set me up with a part-time course in industrial administration alongside a part-time job as a foreman's apprentice at a group joint venture, Tube Investment, UK. This two-year apprenticeship at TI, under an extremely hard taskmaster who was later to become a friend, taught me the value of disciplined work, and got me to understand that a good manager has to walk the talk.

I returned to India and joined the family business. Through my career, I have played a variety of roles wherever the family thought my services would, and could, be utilized. And, so I did everything that the family needed me to do, even when I didn't want to. This was the case when my elders asked me to take up the responsibility of *panchayat* president in our ancestral village, a responsibility I took hesitantly. It turned out to be great learning ground. Many years later, it was a similar scenario when I was deputed to run EID Parry.

It was by mere chance that turnarounds fell into my lot, first Carborundum Universal and then Tube Investment of India, both on a smaller scale than EID Parry (which was to come later) as they were limited to engaging with the government and dealing with labor issues.

If ever a turnaround was needed, it was at EID Parry. When we took over, the company was in complete doldrums, commercially and in terms of its organizational culture. It had been in trouble for more than 20 years before we took it over; making money on the side was rampant. It was a difficult situation, and in such situations I tend to look towards nature for solutions (and it has yet to fail me). So I set to work at EID Parry, intent on taking out the weeds so that the rest could grow. One example of this weeding out process was an early exercise I undertook. I got the senior executive team together and asked them to anonymously put down names of colleagues they thought were corrupt. In spite of a few objections and arguments, this process went through and revealed a 70 percent correlation in those considered corrupt. Resignations followed. This was clearly hard-headed business at work, but hard-headedness that had value roots. The idea here was to purge the environment of all that was bad so that, that which was good could flourish. This is not to say that there was an immediate change; we merely started to lay the groundwork for a more positive work environment.

It is equally important that one walks the talk, even on the small stuff, as that sets the tone and also acts as an organizational binder, call it glue. And so it was on my first day at the Parry corporate office. I entered the building to find that while one elevator had been held up waiting for me—one elevator was designated for senior management only—the other had a long queue of EID staff, 37 to be exact. Representative of a professional caste hierarchy ("us" and "them" identities) which EID of yore had perpetuated, I immediately scrapped the system. Now, in the scheme of things, this may not be a significant assertion, and could well be called cosmetic, but it was a small beginning towards the message that we were trying to send across the company.

Intuition pointed me toward communication. I have been a people person in that I am happy talking to people, be it about their problems or otherwise. Over time, I realized that this stood me in good stead professionally as it developed a level of mutual trust (an attribute I shall return to later), and also provided me insights which ordinarily I might not have access to. I used all opportunities in this attempt, not least among which were my tours to the factories and the branches. Traveling economy class on these flights, I often invited junior colleagues who happened to be traveling with me to sit by me, and tell me about their specific problems and the solutions as they might see them. These interactions enhanced my perspective and possibly helped me in becoming a better manager.

And, so I come to an example from my Parry days. With the company takeover just sealed, I was driving to the company's sugar factory in a Parry car and with a Parry driver. It was a long journey—the factory was 150 kilometers away—during the course of which I attempted to engage the driver in conversation. He was clearly suspicious of me in my takeover *avataar*. Finally, and with some difficulty in gaining a little of his trust, I managed to break the ice. And, it was from him that I got my firsthand peek into what was wrong with the company. He told me about himself, that he was the fourth generation in the service of the company, that he had himself seen the company go down in the previous 20 years, and that everybody was making money—even him! The point of this story is that it is always good to listen to people, not only the generals but more so the troops. By and large, they are the heart of the story.

Communication yields information which is valuable in forming a cogent overall perspective. Once that is clear, one has to assume the role of a facilitator. I have never been an expert on the businesses I have run; hence, I attempted to understand the processes and facilitate others on the operational aspects. This required a level of delegation which I learnt from my eldest brother who was a great Tamil scholar, and was moved by the *Thirukurral*.[1] I quote from a passage from the *Thirukurral* in which Saint Thiruvalluvar writes about employee empowerment: "After having considered [that] this man can accomplish this by these means, let the leader leave with him the discharge of that duty" (Kural 517). My brother understood each and every person and delegated matters according to the person's strength. This ability to delegate intelligently lies at the heart of any successful enterprise.

To facilitate and delegate, one has to trust. It is important to maintain an organizational climate conducive to trust. I am of the firm belief that one has to go in with trust and depend on people; give them a long rope. That said, one has to recognize that trust is a two-way street, and one has to be open to the fact that things can

[1] *Thirukkural*, is a classic of couplets (1,330 rhyming Tamil couplets) celebrated by Tamils. It was authored by Thiruvalluvar, a poet who is said to have lived anytime between the second and sixth centuries AD.

go awry. Business, as life, is a balance of a number of elements. Nowhere does this balance exhibit itself most than in this scenario. The underlay of all that I have said is ethics. I like to believe that our family has strong values and beliefs, most of which emanate from my grandparents, and most of which guide the way we do business even today. Our overarching business value is to adhere to ethical norms in all dealings with shareholders, employees, customers, financial institutions, and the government. We may not have grown as fast as some of our contemporaries, but our reputation with the government, financial institutions, customers, and employees is excellent. This trait may have made us conservative, but that is a path we have chosen to tread.

Walking this path has not been without challenges: in some instances, we have sold verticals when we thought we would be unable to run them or, in others, we chose to fight the system from within.

EID Parry used to manufacture Parry's gin and Caesar's brandy. On taking over the company, we were given to understand that in this kind of business the norm was for every one truck-load that went out of the factory after paying the excise duty, one went without, with the spoils said to be shared among all involved in the transaction. We sold the business.

On the flip side, in 1994, EID was given permission to set up an acetic acid plant at Cuddalore in Tamil Nadu. We set up the factory, only to realize that the permission to set up the factory did not include the permission to transport the basic raw material (that is, alcohol) from the sugar factory to any other location—an action which essentially made the new acetic acid factory redundant. We could have taken the route of greasing palms to facilitate the permission, which might well have been the very purpose of the missing transport permission. We, however, challenged the decision in court. The court gave its ruling: it recognized the state's authority not to grant us the transport permission, but asked the authority to state its reasons. Since there wasn't any, we got the permission! Our point through all of this was that we were willing to hold out for what we thought was correct.

As of now there is no written family constitution (in spite of a few attempts to codify it). Rather, there are a number of unwritten rules, updated over time, which govern the family. The whole family accepts and respects these rules, possibly because they have stood the family and business in good stead till now. These rules govern how we work together, our compensation, the manner in which ownership is passed on from one generation to the next, and who can work for the business. We are one of the very few families to have a retirement "policy" (65 years) and fortunately one of the few which do not have 90-year-old CEOs leading day-to-day operations.

I consider that dialogue is far more important than a written constitution; communication is of the essence. The strain comes in when family members stop communicating with one another. The restrictiveness of a written constitution is also revealed by the fact that certain values cannot be conveyed effectively in writing: for example, how do you state that reputation is more important than money? These values need to be lived if the next generation is to imbibe them—akin to knowledge and culture in India which used to be transmitted from generation to generation through an oral tradition.

My grandfather's unusual view of business extended to a balance between values and profits, and the group's business philosophy can be summed up in the verse from the ancient Indian treatise on wealth creation and governance, the *Arthashastra:* "The fundamental principle of economic activity is that no man you transact with will lose, then you shall not." And, within such a worldview we have set aside 1 percent of profits from all group companies for our family foundation which runs schools and hospitals. Education and health are the two areas we have consistently focused on in terms of our work in the community. And I like to think that all this was much before "corporate social responsibility" became the catch phrase as it is today. The importance of working in the community is possibly best illustrated by another couplet my grandfather was inspired by: "If you build a house and dig a well, the water is available only for your family. But if you build a temple tank (water tower), the whole community can share that water." My grandfather built his house in 1917 and the water tower in 1920. He built the first hospital in 1924. And this is the maxim—return to the community what you get—we have attempted to follow across our business and life. If not shared, wealth and knowledge become useless, as aptly put in perspective by the Tamil word *selvam* (I'll keep going).

Our emphasis on tradition and cultural values notwithstanding, we have not forsaken change. We have always tried to grow through continuous organizational renewal, consistent with our values and beliefs. This is in the belief that if we do not create change ourselves, change will overtake us, thus creating trouble for us. This ability to change is reflected, historically, in the manner in which our business has evolved—from banking to manufacturing to where we are now. It is this constant of change that inspired the separation of ownership from operational management, a process which started in 1999.

Leadership of seven individual companies switched from family members to professional non-family managers, all promoted from within. The family members who had headed these companies moved to a shared office suite and became full-time members of the MCB. They were joined on the board by three independent outsiders—people who represented a variety of business experience: N. S. Raghavan, cofounder of Infosys (and then recently retired); Dr Marti Subrahmanyam, professor of international business finance at the Stern School of Business; and Natalino Duo, an Italian who worked as India's regional managing director for Benetton, a successful family-owned global clothing manufacturer. This significantly important move had been long in the making.

After taking over business leadership of the group in 1996, and after consulting family elders, I requested a prominent business colleague and respected family friend, Dr Ashok Ganguly, to facilitate communication on family business leadership among the family members active in the enterprise. The group met once or twice a month for almost two years to chart the course of change. These meetings threw up five reorganization goals:

1. to be a group rather than a disparate collection of independent entities
2. to be flexible in the makeup of the portfolio of businesses
3. to have less individual attachment to specific businesses
4. to make a shift away from family-led units to non-family-led units
5. to mentor non-family CEOs for the longer-term view

With the operationalization of this change, we became an atypical family business—one that had made an attempt at seamless professionalization in the interests of the business as a whole.

Keeping with the tradition of the family, I retired in February 2004 on reaching the age of 65 years. After my retirement, I went on a sabbatical to the Centre of Family Enterprise at Kellogg School of Management under Professor John Ward. Right at the outset, John queried our family tradition of retiring at the age of 65. I didn't have a ready answer; it dawned on me much later when I returned to India and learnt more about the concept of *Vanaprastha*. This was our family's rationale for retiring from the business at the age of 65.

According to Vedic philosophy, there are four stages of human life: *Brahmacharya*, *Grihastha*, *Vanaprastha*, and *Sanyasa*. While much has been written about three of these stages, the concept of *Vanaprastha* was never fully understood or practiced. The concept was explained by a young Sanskrit scholar in form of a verse which explains the object of this life-stage by a metaphorical comparison of the life of a mango fruit to that of a watermelon. While a fully ripe mango gets damaged either by falling on the ground or being pecked at by a squirrel or a bird, the watermelon, growing near the ground, comes off its stem automatically when fully ripe without getting damaged. A person who is fully mature and has fulfilled all his duties toward the family and business should, hence, be like a watermelon fruit. This means that a person should naturally move from the *Grihastha* life-stage—moving away from the mainstream business—to *Vanaprastha*, when he devotes time to giving back to society.

So, in this context, after my retirement from the Murugappa Group, I decided to take up the role of managing trustee of our family foundation, and I also accepted to be a trustee of the village temple trust as well as village trust. Further, I accepted an invitation by the Ministry of Finance to be the Chairman of a recently formed public–private partnership, National Skills Development Corporation (NSDC), mandated to skill/up-skill 150 million people in India by 2022. In this manner, I hope to give back to society at both ends of the spectrum—community and nation.

In conclusion, I recall the late Professor Pulin Garg's[2] interpretation of the *Shanti Parva* which provides the "philosophical anchors of institution-building."

---

[2] The above quote comes from one of the most famous dialogues on governance and leadership in the Indian lore. It is the advice given by Bhishma (the grand patriarch of the *Mahabharata*) to Yuddhistra (the eldest of the Pandavas, the winners of the epic battle). Professor Pulin K. Garg who taught Organization Behaviour at the Indian Institute of Management (Ahmadabad), summarizes this dialogue in lectures at the Summer Programme (1988) of the Indian Society of Individual and Social Development.

The nature of beauty is in order;
The nature of systems is certainty;
The nature of structure is security;
These define the "oughts" of a good society. When the "oughts" become "musts," they become tools of oppression and unleash great sorrow. When that sad day arrives, the way to regenerate the society is not to defy or to deny but to define; not to resist or to desist but to persist.

One little man in India showed us the way—Mahatma Gandhi. He created history and showed each one of us the way to make our own story by fulfilling our duties—the things we ought to be doing, instead of doing the things we are told we should do.

Chapter 3
_____

The Importance of being "You"

—Adi Godrej

Through the Looking Glass

As I look back, I realize that much of what I needed to know, especially about running a business, I learned as a little boy. My mother, Jai Godrej, was my first—and best—mentor. She taught me about the pride associated with combating fear and, surprisingly enough, turning it into self-reliance—probably the most important and encouraging lesson I have ever learned. I was only five years old when I learned how to cross the road, in front of our Malabar Hills home in Mumbai, on my own. That was the first cornerstone in combating the seemingly daunting unfamiliar.

My first classes in budgeting started shortly thereafter, when I was 10 years old. I was given a fixed amount as an allowance, for my school fees and buying my schoolbooks, toys, and any other needs. I soon learned how to make it work. I count these two initiations into independence among the most influential in my life.

I believe that each one of us is irrevocably shaped by our childhood experiences. These experiences, and the resultant learning, shape the essence of who we are, thus making each story unique. Admittedly, most of this happens unconsciously, and in the process of crafting memories we are subtly molding ourselves. I often find myself looking back at decisions and wondering where the turning points were as I grew up, and many of these answers go back in time.

Growing up at Work

I had known all along that I was going to work in our family business. I was very keen to equip myself with the best possible education before joining Godrej. So, with that aim in mind, in 1959, I joined the Massachusetts Institute of Technology (MIT) and decided to combine my study of engineering with that of management. That was before India became host to the stream of strong management schools that she boasts of today. I was excited and nervous and terribly ambitious as I set out on what was a rather long journey.

At MIT I learned my formative lessons in working together as a team. As a member of the Pi Lambha Phi, a live-in fraternity on campus known for inducting a melee of members from across the globe, I was exposed to tremendous learning on the cultural front. The world as I knew it was unfurling on so many different levels. This was the time to experiment and be a part of all the change that was around me. Back in 1961, we elected Mike Evans, an African-American, as president of that fraternity, a move that was almost unheard of at that time. These were small steps, but they impacted each one of us unmistakably, and we carried a large part of it back with us.

It was in America that I had to push myself really hard to make ends meet, something that I had honestly never known in India. At that time, as per the Government of India norms, you could get only US$210 (₹1,000) a month from India; hence, I had no choice but to work things out for myself. Two of the several part-time jobs I did, as a result of this, greatly impacted me. First, I was lucky enough to work as a research assistant for Franco Modiligani, who was to win the Nobel Prize later for economics in 1985. The exposure was invaluable. Second, I worked as a bellboy and bus boy at a resort hotel, an experience which helped me to understand the importance of service delivery and dignity of labor—values I continue to draw from.

All Eyes on India

I returned to India after completing my studies, after experiencing an experimental West. I was all geared up for making a change at Godrej, be it in the way we embraced our values, or how we honed our management skills. In 1963, when I joined Godrej Soaps, as it was then known, I became the first person trained in management in our company. I quickly immersed myself in working in the "real world," without having any real prior work experience. Fresh and enthusiastic and bursting with ideas, I started out on building our company.

Back then, the Godrej Group was a ₹100 million business and, in retrospect, had a long way to go. Today, some 48 years down the line, we comprise seven major companies with interests in a diverse set of businesses—real estate, fast moving consumer goods (FMCG), industrial engineering, appliances, furniture, security, and agri-care, to name a few—with a turnover in excess of US$3.8 billion. From where we started out as a home-grown Indian brand, we now have a quarter of our revenue coming from our overseas businesses. With 500 million Indian consumers who use a Godrej product every day, we are now counted as one of the five largest groups in terms of consumer reach, headquartered in the developing world.

We could probably never have imagined this rapid pace of growth back then. When I look back on how we have come of age at a juncture where diversity is a byword and the melting pot of cultures an oft-quoted image, I realize that in its own unique way, my tryst with this started somewhat unknowingly at MIT.

One of the biggest strengths I brought to the table back then was not the fancy idea of changing the world, but a perspective into the need to improve upon management practices and handling our people and strategy. We had the engineering skill and excellence comfortably secured, but management was what we needed to build on. I was able to introduce formal financial analysis, marketing, and human resource practices for the first time.

Notes to Myself

I have often been asked about what it takes to be successful—what is the secret winning formula? I don't have a readymade answer to that and I doubt I ever will, but what I do want to share are the personal reminders on my to-do list. I guess you could call these my notes to myself.

THE BUCK STOPS AT ME

Revisiting your core beliefs helps you understand where you come from. The depth of poignant experiences and the learning from them are entrenched in us unmistakably. Your values make you who you are, and let no one tell you otherwise. There are no shortcuts or compromises here. This is one of the things that I learned the hard way, when early on I once chose to brush aside a compromise on values when it came from an otherwise high-performing individual.

As leaders and trendsetters in our own right today, it is our responsibility to constantly evaluate how we stand up for what we believe in. My experiences through the years have taught me the value of discipline, integrity, and the relentless pursuit of excellence. It is what I stand for and what I hope for each person who is touched by Godrej.

I am a firm believer that it all boils down to whether or not you can lead by example. You need to set yourself high standards of personal accountability and to be seen to follow them without compromise, before you start preaching.

Many things will come and go out of style, but never who you are and where you come from. Integrity is a buzzword today, but for me, it has personally always meant more than mere financial probity. Integrity to who you are and what your thoughts, ideas, hopes, and ambitions are—and will become—are more challenging, and I urge you to spend time exploring this. The answers will not always come immediately, but you owe yourself this time and serious input. It will not be easy and you will find yourself repeatedly questioned, but it is for you to fight for this. It is also true that you might not always win; you will fail at times and have to pick yourself up and move on. There can be no simpler or more complicated a truth, for unless you know and believe in your values and where you come from, you will never know where you can reach.

(FAILING) TO LEARN

Sometimes, you just need to put yourself out there and take a risk, knowing that you could possibly fail at it. Failure comes with its own rich set of learning and, if you play it well, it could end up being one of your strongest props. In fact, I believe that learning comes in various guises, and you never quite know when she is going to step out of the shadows and present you with her visiting card.

I have found that whether you approach this as a leader or a teammate or an individual, arguably the best way to learn is by reflecting upon your failures. One of the biggest challenges you could face as a leader is to keep your team geared up to perform to the best they possibly can. How you approach challenging situations, inspire and, at times, even coax your teammates out of disappointments, goes a long way in building your successes.

I often tell a story when we first introduced the concept of 360-degree feedback at Godrej. It was a defining moment for all of us, when this bold new process thrust feedback at us and even pushed us into learning how to accept it. As a part of the feedback from this process, I was told rather bluntly that I was a poor listener, not encouraging feedback from others, arrogant about my ideas, and interrupted people too much when they were speaking. This made me sit up and start thinking long and hard about the kind of leader and colleague that I was coming across, as I believe the worst thing that a leader can do is to not listen.

It is easy to get carried away by blaming systems and processes and people. It is also easy to get angry, but let me share with you that it just does not work that way. If you ever get the impression that any of those reactions helped change a situation, then I can vouch with a fair deal of confidence that the alteration came about in spite of the angry reaction and the blame game and not because of it.

I now try to make it a point to exploit every opportunity that I can to learn from my colleagues and subordinates, my children and even my grandchildren.

SPOILT FOR CHOICE/WHAT IF?

Today, opportunities are in abundance. This generation will probably be remembered, among other things, for the wealth of choice available to it. In fact, I am constantly re-learning how to size and resize opportunities. The pitfall, however, is omnipresent—that of losing oneself in the array of choices and missing a perfectly good opportunity with the thought that a better one would come along.

You need a purpose, a vision, even if it is broad based. Identify milestones; think through what would make you happy and proud, and what it is that you would like to contribute toward. Then work on bringing them to life. I have always attempted to structure my short-term goals with as much clarity and direction as possible, so as to slowly but deliberately, build toward a larger future.

The tricky part is staying balanced on shifting ground. Even as you plan for, and work toward your goal, you will encounter ongoing changes and challenges and probably even opportunities to do something else, and do it better. You need to figure out for yourself what really motivates you and how best to remain grounded and focused. While there are numerous books and expert speak on this, I find my examples closer home in my children and grandchildren and their unique abilities to balance a passion for their legacy with a determined drive for change.

HARDWIRING DISCIPLINE

I have always believed very strongly in the need for discipline. By this I do not mean a creativity-stifling mechanical routine, but the need for generating a structure and patterns. When you are swamped with multiple responsibilities, even as you juggle the varied roles in your life, the trick to succeeding at it lies in how best you can accord each event the attention and importance that it demands. Parent, grandparent, child, sibling, spouse, friend, boss, mentor, and colleague—you wear multiple hats and it is difficult to keep everyone happy.

My days start early—I am at my office by 8 a.m. I fell into this habit early in life when my children were young and had to leave early for school. I used to make it a point to always have breakfast with them before they left. As soon as they left for school, I would leave for work. Another daily routine is to make detailed checklists (a to-do list) of things that have to be done that day. This is something that I have been doing for a long while now and is quite intrinsic to what I have become. One of the biggest opportunities that these little routines have opened up for me is the ability to do so much more with my time.

I guess you could call me a bit of a fitness freak—I do my best to exercise for at least 10 hours a week to stay fit. I have always been fond of sports. When I was young, I used to play a lot of tennis and squash and often went horseriding. Now, I spend most of my time on water sports and prioritize a weekly Sunday water-skiing date with my grandchildren. My other passion is for travel. I enjoy traveling the world and happily juggle business and personal exploration schedules to make the most of the time that I can get.

Having said that, I have also come to realize that it is absolutely okay to stop and ask for help sometimes, even if you think that it makes you look like you can't handle all of it together. It is also okay to say no. I say these both on the work and personal fronts—whether you like it or not, you will have to make choices, so have the discipline to accept that.

Since discipline has always formed such a vital part of my approach to work, I naturally tried to extend it to how we approached our systems at Godrej. In my opinion, one of the most effective ways in which we have hardwired discipline is in the financial prudence that we follow. We use the concept of economic value-added (EVA) to measure the financial performance of our businesses, which is the measure of profits after deducting the cost of capital from profit. This metric has enabled us to be much more disciplined about how we approach capital employed in our businesses and remain focused on returns to our shareholders than we would have been otherwise. Like I have often said, for us sales is vanity, profit is sanity, and cash is reality.

DON'T DOWNSIZE YOUR AMBITION

If you are going to dream, then dream big. You need to keep up the tempo and sustain your passion for work, more so if you are starting out young and have a long way to go. In an increasingly competitive world, you need to have an edge to make your way through it. Networking and leveraging informal working relationships is usually a stumbling block for most of us, so whether there are formal mechanisms or not, I strongly advocate learning how to navigate through these. Be open to experimenting and look for alternatives along nonlinear career paths, if that is what interests you. If you stop challenging yourself, you will just get bored after a while, so look for these alternatives and make them work for you.

If you are doing well and growing fast, then you will soon hit the end of the existing road and be faced with the question of whether or not to stumble into the unfamiliar. I have always found these moments greatly inspirational to me. Teamed with the right advice—my friends have provided wonderful support at such junctures—I have found that they open up great opportunities.

One leadership mantra that I believe in wholeheartedly is that the key lies in thinking about the future backwards, not the present forward. In relation to this, I have always admired Warren Buffet for his sound ability to be able to foretell trends and avoid getting trapped in momentary bubbles of excitement.

For us at Godrej, this is an exciting time of discovery when our 114-year young legacy is gearing to meet India's exciting future as we chart our course to becoming an emerging market multinational. We have recently spent time charting out our future trajectory and have set ourselves ambitious goals, our 10×10 vision—to grow 10 times in 10 years. I believe that we are well positioned to pursue this goal given that we have delivered strong results over the last 10 years and have the funding ability to invest for this growth, clubbed with a rather favorable macroeconomic scenario. However, in order to make this possible, we will need to ensure that we continue to turbocharge talent development, improve R&D effectiveness and the innovation pipeline, and preserve agility and execution focus.

As a group, we have always actively championed social responsibility. We have spent the last year exploring what we can do to further our commitment through "shared value" initiatives that create both social and business benefits. In line with this, we are focused on playing our part in creating a more inclusive and greener India and have named this effort "Godrej Good & Green." As part of our Good & Green Vision, we aspire by 2020 to create a more employable Indian workforce, reach global best standards in environmental sustainability, and innovate for products that address the under-served needs of Indians at the bottom of the income pyramid. I strongly believe that this vision will play a vital role in defining our contributions over the coming decades.

Being optimistic is a clincher as far as I am concerned. Though, admittedly, optimism without a dose of realism is ineffective, one shouldn't hide behind the latter, using it as an excuse to avoid stepping out of the comfort zone. Probably the biggest challenge I have faced as a leader was when we had to take some fundamentally difficult calls on changing our trajectory as a group to respond to emergent India's much-anticipated embracing of liberalization in 1991.

IT TAKES TWO TO TANGO

I learned very soon that my ambitious dreams could not be mine alone. It takes two to tango. If you are working as a team, then you need to collectively own the ideas. For me, teamwork starts with establishing a clear vision and a sense of purpose or identity. This is paramount and cannot be reduced to a cliché. The team should together agree on and shape the future, and I often find myself shuttling between the roles of leader and teammate.

A great example of how we did this at Godrej was our re-branding exercise in 2008, which formulated the "brighter living" vision. This vision was, in fact, the result of intense dialogue and debate with scores of people across our companies.

However, just having a vision is never enough. All stakeholders should have clarity about the vision; if people are confused about what it is directed at and what exactly they are supposed to do with it, then it fails to hold ground. So, we have tried to make sure that the vision is translated into specific performance goals so as to ensure that each team member is aligned to the vision.

You have to work hard to create the right conditions for teamwork. One of my biggest realizations has been that it is imperative to invest time in ensuring that the team gels together. I do my best to create an environment that encourages trust, candid discussions, and collaboration. At Godrej, we also focus on ensuring that our senior management lead by example and act as guides, a philosophy which ties in with our company-wide policy of *bedhadak bolo*, which encourages people to speak up without inhibitions. We also believe very strongly in the need for diversity and "whole-brained" thinking and endeavor to bring together people with diverse skill-sets to build complementary teams.

Over to You

India has come a long way in making her presence felt globally, and we are lucky to be a part of this resurgence. Today's potential and tomorrow's opportunities are what generations before mine could only dream of. As members of the community of an emergent and more global India, we have increasing responsibility toward how tomorrow will shape up.

Our most defining role as leaders will be to demand better and push for more. Societal issues are clearly gaining increased attention with citizens across emerging countries boldly taking a stand, acting as moral police, and voicing their discontentment. Whether it is an oppressive dictatorial regime, growing environmental backlashes or, closer home, the uproar against corruption, the writing on the wall is clear. Success isn't determined by mere economic growth or profit figures; we need to build more sustainable models, complete with irrefutable corporate governance and then live up to them.

Chapter 4

The Turning Points in Our Journey of Transformation

—Kumar Mangalam Birla

At times, life's turning points occur gradually. Sometimes, like lightening, they strike suddenly, a bolt out of the blue. We put it down as a freak occurrence, a Black Swan event, and a hand of fate. There are also those who lean on hindsight to make the case that the disaster was waiting to happen; no one would heed their warning! Sometimes, we are squarely in the eye of the storm and are rocked and buffeted. Sometimes, if we are fortunate, we sail through with minor bruises.

How one fares depends on the responsiveness of individuals and their degree of awareness, powers of observation, and sensitivity to the event. For most of us, if an apple were to fall on our head, we would shrug it off as just one of those things and quickly forget it and turn our attention to other things. But if that same thing happens to Isaac Newton, it results in a totally different course of events. So the same event can affect or shape different people differently.

These turning points have the potential to change the course of individuals, nations, and even civilizations. As we say, if a butterfly flaps its wings in one part of the world, that can well lead to a storm at the other end of the world.

Look at some of the turning points people have been through, and consider how profound the impact of that moment was. When Gandhiji was thrown out of a whites-only train compartment in South Africa, his focus changed forever, from his law career to the struggle for human dignity and equality, leading to India's struggle for freedom from the colonial rule. When Jamshedji Tata was refused entry into a club because he was an Indian, it affected him so much that he resolved to set up a hotel just as grand that would welcome Indians—that led to the Taj. When the tape recorder was invented around the early 1950s, for some time it failed to sell. One day, Akio Morita, the founder of Sony, was walking, and he happened to see a man in an antique shop handing over a lot of money to buy a vase, which cost much more than a tape recorder and had much less utility. That was one of the turning points for him. At that moment, he decided that Sony must communicate aggressively the applications and benefits of the product to get people to buy it. So he went to the law courts, which were experiencing a shortage of stenographers. Eureka! That was when everything changed. These momentous turning points strike every industry. The advent of word processing revolutionized not only the type-writer industry, but also workplace practices—now even managers and professionals can, and have to, do a large part of their typing themselves.

It's not just individuals that experience turning, but nations and the world do too. The assassination of Archduke Franz Ferdinand, heir to the Austro-Hungarian throne, triggered a chain of events that led to World War I. The fall of the Berlin Wall was another such turning point. In India, the balance of payments crisis in 1991, when India had to pledge its gold holdings, turned out to be a major turning point that led to the unleashing of economic reforms.

While learning is a continuous, life-long process, during major turning points the intensity and force of learning takes a quantum leap. Learning becomes intense and compressed. For me, every inflection point has turned out to be a powerful period of learning. It's like an exploding star that emits a lot of light within a short burst of time.

At such times, learning is driven deeply into you, by the force of circumstances. These are the times when great upheavals are experienced, be they in personal life, at work, in your industry, or in the global economy. Sometimes they come in the shape of headwinds, sometimes as tailwinds. Each of those moments is a moment of truth. When you are passing through the eye of the storm, you are wonderfully focused, because often, this can be a make or break moment.

Let me now recount some of the key turning points that I, personally, and our Group have been through over the years, and what we learned from those moments. These turning points are not always sequential. Neither are they strictly points—they can be an extended period. Often, there are different forces at work at the same time. And sometimes one turning point leads to another. So one cannot always neatly demarcate the cause and the effect.

Turning Point 1: Passing Away of My Father

On a personal note, the biggest turning point for me was the death of my father. It was a very difficult time emotionally because my father passed away unexpectedly. Also because of the large responsibility that I had to suddenly shoulder. At that time, I was pretty much in a fish bowl. I was only 28, while the average age of the Group was 56. Filling in the shoes of a legendary icon was a tough ask. I had limited but high quality experience and exposure under him.

But at that point in time the only thought in my mind was to carry forward my father's work, his legacy of creating wealth for our multiple stakeholders. So I decided that I'd just put my head down, hang in there, and just keep going at it. Truthfully, I was much better prepared than most people thought because of a couple of factors. When you grow up in a business family, subconsciously there is a lot of learning that happens. It might just be conversations across the dinner table, for example.

Moreover, I had worked with my father for seven–eight years before he passed away. He had given me independent charge of a few of our plants. I had sat with him very closely for his meetings and kind of shadowed him for four years. I learnt how to be adept in dealing with different business situations. So I wasn't a rookie. When the mantle of the business fell on me, for the initial years, I worked late into the night, seven days a week, kept up crazy schedules, listened a lot, asked a lot of questions, and encouraged constructive discussions. I was never a fence sitter.

The passing away of my father was not only a turning point for me. It was one of the key defining moments for our Group. He was a huge store of energy, drive, inspiration, and charisma. His passing away created a void that had to be quickly filled, as best we could. I can tell you firsthand that a leadership transition of the type we had to engineer can be one of the most traumatic periods in the life of an organization. I was, however, fortunate to have the emotional support, goodwill, and backing of a solid team. It was a great business and organizational legacy that my father had left me. That's what made the task manageable and doable. So one of the lessons was the importance of the emotional connect of people. I was fortunate to be able to dip into the deep pool of goodwill built up over decades, and that made all the difference.

Another important lesson for me was the criticality of building great teams. We, in India more than elsewhere, tend to be very individualistic. This is partly an outcome of our educational system, which necessitates cutthroat competition. It puts a premium on individual achievement and brilliance, at the cost of team or organizational effectiveness. Although individual stars are valuable, they cannot, by themselves, create the brilliance of a galaxy.

In business, one constantly has to interact with people and work in teams. Most business situations cut across a range of product, geographic, and functional areas. Hence, a full range of competencies needs to be deployed to deal with the situation at hand. No one person has all the answers. Naturally, teams are the predominant and most effective setting for carrying out complex tasks.

At different points in time, depending on needs of the business, one may have to be engaged with multiple teams, move out of one team, and connect with a new one. This calls for skills in multitasking, as well as an ability to repeatedly make on and off mental and emotional switches. The textbooks have yet to ink out ready answers to how best these real-world skills can be learnt.

Turning Point 2: Unleashing of India's Liberalization

While the unleashing of India's liberalization process in 1991 was indeed a turning point for our country and business houses, it took a while for the reforms to get rooted. By 1995 the reforms were being aggressively pushed. Very soon after my sudden transition from an entry-level apprentice to a CEO, I sensed that our Group needed to change. The changing business landscape called for new thinking, new ideas, and new attitudes. We had to move away from a mindset that was based on decades of monopoly, to one based on a future in which competitive pressures would be increasing across every business. That would call for large-scale development of people, as well as induction of talent from outside.

These compulsions were completely at odds with the way the Group functioned then. There was an implicit guarantee of lifetime employment, lack of ethnic diversity, and under-representation of women. We lacked the brand image and reputation to attract young talent from the leading educational institutes. I remember a pre-placement talk I was giving at the Indian Institute of Management (IIM) Calcutta (now Kolkata). At the end of it, I asked how many students would like to join our Group. Not a single hand went up. They did not like the fact that we did not have a retirement policy and that the Group was hierarchical, that it lacked training and development processes for the young. There was little differentiation—in recognition and rewards—between performers and nonperformers. The alarm bells had begun ringing.

I sensed that we needed a transformation—not a cosmetic transformation, but a fundamental change in the way we operated. I believe transformation is all about turning aspirations into reality. It is about converting setbacks into opportunities. But I had the courage of conviction. To me, transformation is about what Charles Handy calls "the creation of new alchemists from ordinary people".[1] Admirably supported by our HR Director, Dr Santrupt Misra, and others on the Management Team, we set up highly energized processes. We were firm in our belief that we had

[1] Charles Handy. 1999. *The New Alchemists*. UK: Hutchisnson.

people with an indomitable spirit who would help us make new things happen and create value. The only question was: when? The timing needed to be worked out carefully.

I had to take the skeptics and doubters along. Very often, the approach of building a consensus puts a break on speed at a particular point. But if I look back along the entire change cycle, consensus usually speeded the process. Once people are on the same wavelength, the problems at the implementation stage are dramatically fewer, the resistance much less. Things move forward at a faster clip. I believe that it helps to have individuals and teams involved in the decision-making process. Once they own the idea, the commitment to the task at hand is much greater. There is no attempt to push the blame and there is no looking back.

Today when I mull over our Group's transformational journey over these 17 years, I believe that we have changed in very fundamental ways. In fact the genetic coding of our Group stands altered substantially. We have become a global, multicultural entity, comprising more than 133,000 people, drawn from 42 nationalities. More than 60 percent of our people are under the age of 40. Seventeen years ago women executives were few and far between. Today, women constitute more than 17 percent of our managerial cadre, and the number is on the rise.

Today, we are rated as a meritocratic organization, one where talent always bubbles to the top. The Group has been ranked number four in the Global "Top Companies for Leaders" survey and ranked number one in Asia Pacific for 2011. "Top Companies For Leaders" is the most comprehensive study of organizational leadership in the world conducted by Aon Hewitt, Fortune Magazine, and RBL (a strategic HR and Leadership Advisory firm).

As we venture into new countries, our Group's geography has changed phenomenally as well. The work ethos has changed because the world around us has changed dramatically.

So a key learning for us is to continue to constantly reinvent ourselves. Change is the only constant in life.

Turning Point 3: Major Shifts in the Group Strategy

The sharp change in our Group's growth strategy has been a critical turning point. Earlier, we had been growing organically. Our decision to step on the inorganic growth accelerator has been dictated by the fact that some of our businesses demand that we become global players. Hence, fast-forwarding our growth and market position with well-considered acquisitions seemed logical.

In the last 17 years, we have made around 26 acquisitions, in India and overseas. Among them are Novelis (Canada), Mount Gordon and Nifty Copper Mines (Australia), Liaoning Carbon Black (China)[2] and, of course, UltraTech from L&T, Indal from Alcan, Madura Garments from Coats Viyella, among others. Each acquisition has been a learning experience for us. The process of integrating the acquired units with the rest of the organization has

---

[2] Columbian Chemicals (US), Domsjo Fabriker (Sweden), Terrace Bay Pulp Mill (Canada), EYA Star Cement (UAE).

taught us a lot. We have never been a great believer in a mechanistic 30 or 100-day integration plan. On the softer side, our learning has been that each acquisition is unique in its own way. Trying to force fit every M&A into a single mold, never works. At the end of the day, M&As are not about stronger balance sheets or enhanced market shares. Rather, they are about the coming together of people, their hearts and minds, and cultures and values.

Of all our acquisitions, the US$6 billion acquisition of Novelis was among the largest by an Indian company at that time. It moved us several notches higher in terms of scale, global reach, and forward integration. Despite the inherent long-term rationale of the acquisition, over the short term, we had to contend with the attendant higher risks. This stemmed from the funding we resorted to for the acquisition, and also from the onset of the US recession, around the same time we made the acquisition. We were severely criticized, and Hindalco's stock took a temporary beating. Even so, in my gut, I felt it was absolutely the right decision. Yes, we could have bought it cheaper, had we bought it now. But that's hindsight. You cannot time the market. Today, the performance of Novelis has vindicated our decision. Bear this in mind—the Novelis acquisition was done not only by applying our analytical and logical thought processes, but just as importantly by also applying intuition, gut feel, and the sixth sense.

Corporate strategy and acquisitions have been subjects of great attention in the world of management. Here, we did break ranks with the prevailing management thinking that frowned on the conglomerate model of business organization. Our Group had developed as a classic so-called conglomerate. It had proven successful. We found no compelling reason to turn back on something that had worked so well, at least in India. So our thinking was: if it isn't broke, there is no need to throw it away.

However, while retaining the conglomerate model, we did realign and fine-tune our approach in fundamental ways. Most important, we decided that each of our businesses must have the potential to achieve a leadership position in the industry it is in. If that was not feasible, we would exit the business. We exited a few businesses, among them refining, sponge iron, and seawater magnesia. Divesting a business is a difficult thing to do. You have to be careful and not let ego come in the way. Then there are the people—it's wrenching to see the disappointment and the parting with the Group. Generally, though, we negotiated with buyers so that the long-term interests of the business and the employees were taken care of.

A major learning has been about building brand equity globally. Let me recount our experience in acquiring a pulp mill in the New Brunswick province in North Eastern Canada in 2006. The mill—which had been shut for a year—had 400 employees, a large number by Canadian standards. It had run into deep financial trouble. When we first thought of acquiring the mill, it appeared unviable, unless the employees accepted new work norms, unless the union extended complete flexibility and cooperation, and unless the provincial government made significant concessions. There were many constituencies to convince and carry along.

We had to introduce ourselves, tell them our story, and narrate to them our successes and experiences in other countries time and again. This involved talking to individual provincial leaders, making short presentations to leadership teams, and even to the provincial parliament. We met with limited success initially. We had to go back again and again, with more facts, with more evidence, and with more conviction.

The entire community's economic existence in the mill township of Nackawic depended on how credible our revival plans were. While they already knew enough and more about us having searched the Internet, we had to get our story across to the employees, their families, and even to the small business owners in the township. We showed them films on our factories, gave them literature on our company, and answered their searching questions. And, our team did so with sincerity, respect, and a sense of commitment.

Finally, at the end of it all, an Indian company had put a new footprint on Canadian soil. Today, many of the employees feel that they are better off with an Indian MNC that is credible rather than with a local company that had presided over its closure.

So, building brand equity in new economies and winning the confidence of your new stakeholders, despite the strengths you have in your country, is a challenge that can be a humbling experience.

As we shifted to inorganic growth, we have also learnt a great deal about managing acquisitions. One clear lesson is the importance of taking the affected people—employees, their families, suppliers, community leaders, government officials, and politicians, into confidence and keeping the lines of communication open every step of the way. We have, in the process, evolved a very different, non-Anglo-Saxon approach to acquisitions, one that is nonhostile and results in minimum disruption. We usually have little inclination to make drastic changes, overhaul management, retrench people, or close plants. That's not our style. In fact, when we acquired Novelis, the employees there were waiting, almost expecting, that we would take some drastic steps during the process of integration. They were absolutely surprised that nothing earth-shaking happened. Today, Novelis is run by pretty much the same team that was there earlier, and their autonomy is intact. Employees in the West find this approach refreshing.

Turning Point 4: Rapid Increase in the Group's Diversity

Discontinuities, more often than not, turn out to be turning points, for organizations as well as individuals. In our case, the Group's increasing diversity turned out to one such marker of discontinuity. Although this is really an outcome of our strategic shifts, I think it's appropriate to treat this separately as it deals with the important issue of changing mindsets.

Our Group has undergone a huge transformation, from one that was relatively homogenous to one that is strikingly diverse. The diversity is evident whichever way you look.

Earlier, our presence was primarily in traditional industrial businesses. Today, our portfolio has a significant component of new businesses, among them financial services, telecom, retail, branded apparel, and business process outsourcing (BPO).

Many of our businesses are also much more integrated than they were—for instance, in VSF and Metals, we have resorted to acquisitions in order to secure our raw material supplies.

Today our businesses are also much closer to the end customer. For instance, in financial services, retailing and garments, we make direct contact with the final customer. This is a big change from two decades ago.

Turning Point 5: The Great Global Economic Disruption of 2008

Let me mention a fifth turning point. A powerful moment of truth for our Group, as for many other businesses the world over, was the global economic crisis that hit in late 2008. The suddenness, ferocity, and the unexpectedness of it all snowballed into a global recession. In India, we were fortunate to experience only a slowdown over two to three quarters. But more significant than the limited business impact, the crisis forever changed our organization's mindset in very profound ways. This was the closest brush with disaster, in our lifetime and in our memory.

The severe economic and business storm of the type we have flown through is a great litmus test about how strong and valid our strategy is. We now ask ourselves one simple question: If a down-turn of this magnitude were to persist for some time, would we be the last man standing, which means, will we be the industry player least likely to be affected or the least affected? If the answer is yes, our strategy stands the test.

Being a global group, we could not remain unscathed by the crisis. We had to take timely steps to respond to the crisis. For us, that was a time to pause, rethink, and regroup. During the early months of the crisis, the focus was on consolidation and on the basics, such as lowering the break-even point, bolstering cash flow, and cutting the flab.

While, hopefully, the world is past the low point of the crisis, the aftershocks keep rumbling intermittently—an all too familiar phenomenon. It will be a while before the calm returns.

The crisis earlier or even today has not shaken our longer-term strategy. Becoming more efficient is only part of the equation. Few businesses become great just by cutting costs or downsizing. If only it were that simple! Over the long run, what counts is building a robust strategic architecture, innovation, creativity, customer orientation, and the readiness to take risks, all backed by a great team of talented and totally committed people.

We constantly remind ourselves that our objective is to build businesses for the long haul—and I am talking about the next 30, 40, and 50 years. In the past too, there have been sharp swings in business cycles, and there will be more of these in the future, though hopefully, not of the magnitude and ferociousness we witnessed.

A key learning has been the importance of values and beliefs. Our values always guide us, much like the North Star. Our history and heritage as a group, in one word, stand for trust. Whilst we saw a meltdown the world over, not just of economies, but equally of governance, I believe that our demanding standards of governance will set us apart, even more, now, and in the future. Clearly, investors and employees will appreciate and learn to differentiate between organizations like ours that are honest, ethical, transparent, and well governed, and others, for whom governance is merely a platitude. This is a huge strength, ingrained over time into our genetic coding.

Conclusion

At the end of the day, I believe, leadership is all about plugging into the minds and hearts of people. It is about rallying them around to a compelling and exciting vision of the future. It is about upping the quality of imagination of the organization. It is about encouraging a spirit of intellectual ferment and constructive dissent so that people are not bound by the status quo, and mavericks are given space and free play. It is about building the highest levels of empathy, without compromising on fairness and without running a popularity contest.

The most important thing is to dream audaciously, and to pursue that big dream with all the passion and the fire within you. It's about reaching for that dream, no matter what and riding even the most gigantic waves of turbulence and disruption, much like a champion surfer.

Chapter 5

Imprints of the Past and What It Will Take to Succeed in the Future

—Deepak Parekh

M anagement is about doing things right; leadership is about doing the right thing as Stephen R. Covey observed, "Management is efficiency in climbing the ladder of success; leadership determines whether the ladder is on the right wall."[1]

From chiefs of tribes to CEOs of complex corporations, leadership has defined success or failure of the enterprise. Not surprisingly, leadership has been a much debated issue—not only in

[1] Stephen R. Covey. 1990. *The Seven Habits of Highly Effective People*. Free Press.

contemporary times but earlier too. This energetic debate could also be a function of the fact that leaders have been and continue to be in short supply. Why is this so? What is it about leadership that makes its good practice so rare? Is it situation specific? Are there endless varieties of leadership to suit every eventuality? What qualities in a "good" leader inspire and encourage followers to follow? These, and more, have been questions at the center of leadership theory for many years.

Contemporary leadership theory and practice has to work in a changing and increasingly complex global environment, one which puts different demands on leaders and the quality of leadership. This environment requires qualities of leadership which, I believe, are significantly different from those required two decades ago.

This changing global environment is characterized by one overarching fact: globalization. And, this overarching fact has been facilitated by a number of factors and events—increased connectivity at reasonable cost made possible by technological advances; the flow of capital; the choice of global spaces within which to produce; the use of labor markets worldwide without the necessity of migration; the virtual costless availability of information. All this has overturned our conventional notions of both the speed and the manner in which we interact and transact. Wireless telephony, satellite positioning, intelligent computing, robotics are all creatures of the last decade of the 20th century. Gone are the days of certainty and anticipation; welcome to an era of uncertainty and continuous and accelerating flux.

There has been a certain democratization with a leveling of the playing field. The big and established face a significant challenge from the small and the innovative. This changed situation requires different sets of skills, primarily the ability to harness new knowledge and technology for organizational growth and success, be it in the financial services sector or in manufacturing or services broadly defined. The information age necessitates the ability of analysis, and identifying and analyzing the probable consequences of underlying trends will be extremely important if change is to be managed properly. Predicting the future will become crucial, more so than ever before. Peter Drucker has gone much further and proclaimed that "The future has already happened."[2] What he means, of course, is that we need to use the information at hand, identify those events that have strong predictable consequences, and then try and understand them as a means of preparing for the future. Those who can do that accurately and then execute their strategies appropriately pass the test of true leadership.

Leadership is all about moving ahead with two basic instruments: the compass and the clock. One which confirms the direction you are moving in and the other which tells you how fast you will get there. The key question to ask is: do we have the clock and the compass handy with us in our organizations all the time? To have just one is somewhat of a disaster as direction without a

---

[2] Peter Drucker. 2005. "The Future That Has Already Happened (Economic Effects of Underpopulation in Developed Countries)", *The Futurist*. World Future Society.

sense of progress is hollow, and progress—setting budgets, stressing time management, and chasing after them in different time periods—might just get us to the wrong place. Leadership is essentially the ability to visualize the future, to create mental maps of possibilities, to create an enabling environment and conditions. In other words, it means the ability to invent the future, to follow a path that is distinct, and avoiding u-turns.

Let me illustrate this with my own organizational example. For the first 14 years of HDFC's existence, we faced a controlled environment, but we refused to be subservient to it. Developing the organization "as if" we faced a competitive world, we chose to be market oriented on both sides of our balance sheet: resource mobilization as well as lending. This was our vision of a dynamic organization, which put the customer first, even though the external environment did not yet demand it at that time, and was the secret of our success when the external environment changed so rapidly. In effect, what it did was to create an organizational discipline which was outward focused (customers and markets) and, hence, it created perforce a managerial dynamism, automated systems, and a very strong distributional network at a time when we could develop it at leisure not being constrained by the exigencies of immediate pressures. In sum, without having thought it through systematically at the time, we seem to have done exactly the right thing—we concentrated our attention on the customer in terms of product design, pricing and delivery, building an internal discipline and culture, which single mindedly pursued processes through its people.

Competition itself, when it emerged in the mid-1990s, demonstrated to us the slack in our own systems despite our "as if" approach. It illustrated that even if intentions are well placed, there is no force like direct competition to sharpen the saw and to create more focused strategies based on the changing market conditions.

As the barriers between markets and institutions collapsed in the liberalization period, new opportunities opened up and institutions had to redefine their future business. We came to the conclusion that we would stick to our own competitive advantage and diversify using our strengths. This was keeping in mind the fact that HDFC introduced the concept of retail finance in India long before anyone else had ventured into this territory. We redefined our role as providers of retail financial services using our vast distribution strengths of around 25,000 deposit agents apart from our branch network and the distribution strengths of our group companies as well. The HDFC network of institutions was to serve every segment of the retail financial services market using a common organizational culture and techniques but through separately managed entities run by the best possible human resources. It was a rapid and substantial response to changing circumstances.

But it wasn't just about markets and our place in them. It was also about re-engineering, a buzz word which for us simply meant dramatically improving our operating systems to serve customers even better than before. At HDFC, "service" is treated as a product, and it affects everything we do. Our vision is to introduce a participatory process of management by all involved in different activities to redesign the management of our products with a view to constantly improving standards of service to our customers. This involves redesigning office layouts, work flows, automation, product design, and procedures—in effect, everything that affects product delivery to the customer. It also ensures that our philosophy is well understood by the entire organization simply because they are very much part of the process of change. Finally it never stops. The process is constant and ingrained; it forces the organization to constantly scan the environment in relation to internal processes always striving to maintain a better fit at the interface.

Let me also hasten to add that there is no best way of doing things and what I have said reflects somewhat our approach at HDFC. Much of it has arisen from intuition rather than theory—I am happy that what we have done seems to fit with what we ought to have done.

Qualities of Leadership

The quality of leadership is of paramount importance precisely when leaders are initiating new departures, building new companies, identifying new markets, attracting new people, and managing new teams.

VALUES AND PRINCIPLES

Building organizations in the future will require a **strong sense of** purpose and values. Principle-centered leadership seems to me to be fundamental to business leadership in the future. A vision provides a sense of direction on the basis of an assessment of the present, the past, and the likely future, and constitutes an absolute essential for a successful leadership role. Visions, however, can be wrong and hopelessly off the mark if they are not born from strong values, strengthened, and nurtured by an analytical ability to constantly assess emerging environments and strategic alternatives.

Principles of right action define the very core of our leadership philosophy. HDFC, since its very first day of operations, has been a principle-centered organization, or, as Stephen Covey might say, an organization that has been built on the basis of fairness, kindness, efficiency, and effectiveness. We gradually built trust between people, and then empowered them, strengthened communication, and encouraged a participative management style. Trust is the cement of meaningful relationships and an open and creative management style. Without trust and empowerment we could not have built a learning and adaptable organization. The reputation we enjoy today is the result of years of dedication to the principles of right action which have been sensed and enjoyed by so many over so long a period.

ABILITY TO BUILD LONG-TERM RELATIONSHIPS

Integrity in the form of genuineness of purpose and transparency in execution—major building blocks at HDFC—enable strong stakeholder relationships, which are essential in the increasingly volatile marketplace. This encourages true participation with constituents who, specifically for us at HDFC, have been our employees, investors, depositors, and borrowers.

The quality of these relationships not only defines the future prospects for business growth but develops brand loyalty in an otherwise opportunistic environment. HDFC has always taken the long view and shunned short-termism and expediency. Integrity so defined is perhaps the very core of measuring worth—organizational or personal—for without it, we live in delusion and are condemned to sink deeper into self-seeking behavior.

FOCUS ON SERVICE MANAGEMENT

Service has largely been a reactive activity; very rarely proactive when the environment did not specifically demand it. It has rarely been seen as a strategic choice in a competitive world, which is probably why service management as a clearly defined field of systematic study has only recently emerged.

HDFC has been proactive on service from day one. It defines not only what we do, but how we do it. We at HDFC have attempted to ensure that all that we do is anchored in our basic philosophy of service to our customers, be they investors or consumers of our services. Service defines our products, delivery processes, internal systems, and how we interact with ourselves as an organization. Service management with all its connotations has been systematically built over the years and the endeavor continues.

INTUITION

Leadership is not born out of scientific study. It is built out of intuition through understanding the environment around you and how to manage within it. The objective part is normally enveloped with an uncanny intuitiveness for what lies ahead.

Great leaders have had all these qualities in ample supply. When we look at successful organizations, we know that there is outstanding leadership behind them born from a combination of these attributes. These leaders will be different from the leaders of yore. They will be people of ideas who are willing to back them with commitment and energy; they will be young, bright, innovative, risk takers, those willing to take ideas and put them into action. Charles Handy in his book *The New Alchemists* profiles a number of individuals who have created a newer vision of tomorrow, and says, "Today, more than ever, we need more such alchemists in society, at all levels and in all sectors. They sow the seeds of the future. Innovation and creativity, enterprise and entrepreneurship are the vogue words for the new millennium."[3] The characteristic traits of the new alchemists are the 3Ds: Dedication, Doggedness, and Difference, and the first two are nothing without the third.

[3] Charles Handy. 1999. *The New Alchemists*. UK: Hutchinson.

India desperately needs these new alchemists in all sectors. Our entire operating environment should do everything to encourage them. (One could argue that those that do emerge do so against heavy odds.) Till recently in India, wealth was associated with painstaking development of manufacturing—the Tatas, Birlas, and Reliance. The new wealth creators are the new breed of entrepreneurs who two decades ago, could not have dreamt of their success, such as it has been. Peter Drucker says, "The only policy likely to succeed (in the long years of profound changes) is to try to make the future."[4] These new wealth creators have made the future in their respective business.

It is my strong belief that in the Indian context the new leader will be one with impeccable traditions of integrity in thought and deed, a strong sense of history, an understanding of change, an ability to read the subtext of the times, and an agent of change. Success in India is a struggle of the hurdle economy where 5x energy is required to produce x (quite the reverse in most modern societies). The true leader is one who can counter this framework, and, like an ice breaker, cut through pack ice, and create a channel for others to follow. He must have a machine to undertake that task; the inspiration, patience, and optimism to drive it and the energy to sustain it over long periods of time. There are many amongst us with those qualities. Would it not be more sensible to

---

[4] Peter F. Drucker. 2001. *Management Challenges of the 21st Century*. Harper-Business.

cut the hurdles and considerably reduce the challenge for finding Herculean leaders to drive change?

Let me say as a final thought that success in the Indian context should be re-appraised very carefully. In periods of transition, past success is no pointer to future well being. It is the understanding of success that will be crucial—why have we been succeeding, and what will it take to succeed in the future? I like to think that I have been asking myself that question all the time.

Chapter 6

The Audacity of Ambition

—Raghav Bahl

Entrepreneurship called me. I was impelled toward it. There is no other explanation for a guy without a family background in business or the endowment of capital choosing the rough and tumble of enterprise, forsaking the comfort of a well-paying financial job in a multinational corporation with a strong chance of eventually heading the Indian operations.

I was born into an upper-middle class family. My father was an officer of the Indian Administrative Service (IAS). I grew up in Delhi like any bureaucrat's child. I lived in a government house in leafy Chanakyapuri, went to St Xavier's School, and then to St Stephen's college.

After graduation, I was tempted to take a stab at the entrance examination to the Indian Institute of Technology, like my peers, but pulled out at the last minute. My father wanted me to join the Indian Foreign Service, perhaps to vicariously fulfill his own unrequited ambition to be a diplomat. My heart was not in government service, and I withdrew from the IAS prelims. I wanted life outside the narrow confines of technology and the stifling corridors of bureaucracy. My father accepted my decision with grace and assured me of support in whatever I did.

I joined Delhi University's Faculty of Management Studies and obtained an MBA. My first job was with the audit and consulting firm AF Ferguson & Company. Later, I joined American Express. But my heart was elsewhere. I was happier being with people and dealing with popular concerns. I was fond of public speaking. In college, I used to anchor programs like Youth Forum on Doordarshan. Out of it, I did a stint with Newstrack, a stinging monthly video news magazine—India's first—which shot to fame in the days before satellite broadcasting by exposing the violence that Haryana Chief Minister Om Prakash Chautala unleashed during the bye-elections he was contesting. What was a hobby and a passion became life's calling. Like I said, it was ordained.

Entrepreneurship gives play to many talents. One has to understand—and manage—markets, people, finance, technology, trends, and government policy. It demands self-discipline and the ability to stay the course in the face of adversity. It requires a strong belief in oneself. There are rewards too: achievement and the joy of creating wealth. But would I be any kind of entrepreneur?

Would I have set up a power company or a car factory? No. I do not think those turn me on. I am wedded to media. Its intellectual content excites me. I saw opportunity in ideas and the ability to spin them off profitably.

Fortunately, I got into business when India was at the cusp of change. Many years of inward-looking policies had made the economy uncompetitive and broke. The country had no option but to open itself up to foreign investment. Information and communication technologies were seeing radical changes. This was quite pronounced in the media industry. The print medium had moved from hot metal to phototypesetting to desktop publishing. Black and white television had gone color; broadcasting had jumped from terrestrial transmitters to satellites, beyond the control of governments, raising aspirations and changing lifestyles. With the globalization of finance, money was chasing intellectual capital. People with ideas and the ability to execute them could find investors to back them. In India, the software industry showed the way for the media industry to follow. The group that I was to establish would not only be a child of reforms, but also a mirror to them.

Enterprise means ambition. Some bite as much as they can chew. I like to punch well above my weight. It is also a need of the business I am in. The media is no place for the faint-hearted.

From being a production house supplying programs to BBC World, Star TV, Doordarshan, and Sony, the group that I preside over has become the biggest television news network in the country with a bouquet of 25 channels, straddling news and entertainment,

English and Indian languages, print and Internet. We realized in 2005 that we had no choice but to scale up and diversify, and do it fast. I sensed that if we remained small, the chances of becoming irrelevant or being cast away to the fringes were very high. The media industry intrinsically needs size, linkages, and infrastructure to integrate audiences and geographies. A single newspaper, a single edition, a single magazine, or a single channel is nothing.

Atrophy sets in without muscle. To survive we had to grow. I could have continued to be a niche player in business television news. CNBC-TV18 was the leading brand, with considerable influence. I could have chosen safety and control over growth. The choice that a leader makes determines the future of an enterprise. It might die trying to grow. But I had to give it a shot.

Zee had 20 channels, Star 15, and Sony had as many. In the print media industry, the *Times of India* had many newspapers and multiple editions. So in the seven years from 2005, we went from one channel to 25, entered print media, Internet news, films, home shopping, and e-commerce. It took 12 years for us to grow from zero to ₹1,000 million and just half that time to bulk up 35 times over to ₹35,000 million.

To our surprise, everything we tried, clicked. Almost all our brands are number one or two. CNN-IBN, IBN7, Colors, ibnlive. com, moneycontrol.com, in.com, Viacom18, Homeshop 18, and *Forbes India* have all flourished. But the flip side of rapid growth is cash burn. All these brands were in the investment phase and couple of years away from being profitable. When we began the expansion drive, the capital markets were booming. The combined value of our companies listed on the stock exchanges was ₹60,000 million. By selling 10–20 percent of their equity, we thought we could secure about ₹15,000 million to finance our investments.

But the global financial crisis struck us like lightning, and our plans to raise equity evaporated in a flash. Suddenly success became a burden. We were staring at an investment plan of ₹30,000 million. Our brands were strong; they had great embedded value. But we had a debt of ₹20,000 million. It was pulling down the value of our stocks. Investors were unhappy.

This is when another opportunity walked into us. The Telugu media baron, Mr Ramoji Rao, had put his Eenadu channels on the block. While we were successful with our national networks, we realized that regional networks could deliver us audiences with the spending power that advertisers were looking for. Our competitors, Zee and Star, had expanded in that space. It would have taken us about seven years to develop the footprint that Eenadu had if we began anew. I did not let distress cloud my judgment. We made a bid for the Eenadu channels.

I have grown as an entrepreneur through partnerships. That is how an enterprising ideas' man makes up for the lack of capital. When I won the contract for India Business Report on BBC World, India Show on Star TV and Business AM on Doordarshan, I turned to Mr Ashok Advani of the *Business India* group. Since then I have had many partners. For the Eenadu acquisition, I approached Mr Mukesh Ambani. I have known him for many years. Through my interactions, I have developed enormous respect for him. He is a visionary. He also has an endearing ability of being straightforward and honest. I was comfortable doing a transaction with him. Importantly, he was willing to invest without demanding control in return. He could see that the deal with us was a good investment. Reliance Industries needed content for its 4G services, which we could supply. With the government making digitization of satellite signals mandatory, cable operators will not be able to under-report viewership figures, certainly not as much as they now do. Increased subscription revenue can turn the television industry profitable. Mr Ambani's investment enabled us to become free of debt and acquire 12 regional channels. These will drive our next phase of growth.

The gossip networks went viral after that deal. There was much talk that it was just a matter of time before ownership of our network would change hands. I have learnt over the years that it is very important to be open and transparent. It is a leadership tenet with me. Anything left hidden becomes fodder for speculation. It is best to let it all hang out, say exactly as it is. Make the documentation public to secure the confidence and support of shareholders, regulators, and employees. Not everyone will agree. Some will never be convinced. That is life. Leadership is not a popularity contest. If you are convinced, press ahead. A leader has to be a contrarian. They should be able to go against the flow.

Network 18 is one of the few, if not the only group, in the world to have partnerships with iconic and rival American media brands. We are franchisees of CNBC and CNN. *Forbes* is our print media partner. Viacom18 has a relationship with us in the entertainment space. The logic of the business determines whether we should build, acquire, or license a brand.

In the world of finance where borders are porous, the twitch of the Dow, disturbances on Arab Street, the flutter of bonds yields in a south European country, or a dry spell in American fields, can have a ripple effect on our stock markets and the wider economy. Access to international news, footage, reporters, and commentators can enable our audience to make money, cut losses or just look wise. This is where our tie-ups with CNBC and CNN come in. For our viewers moving across countries, they are fixed point of reference. And there are brands we have built like CNBC Awaaz, Homeshop18, or our biggest one, Colors.

Government policies do not allow us to build globally recognized media brands. Politics rather than economic logic determine the restrictions on foreign direct investment. In entertainment television, foreign investment can go up to 100 percent. In news, it cannot exceed 26 percent. If the intention is to retain control in Indian hands, why cannot the limit be raised to 49 percent? There is a further requirement in news broadcasting and publishing that the controlling shareholder should own 51 percent of the equity. This is a draconian provision, especially for a first-generation entrepreneur without legacy capital. It is discriminatory too. In telecoms, which is as sensitive an industry, the only condition is that the chief executive officer and the board are Indian.

These two provisions constrict the balance sheets of media companies. To grow we have had to pile on debt and plough back the profits. As an enterprise leader, I have had to do financially imprudent things and also look for growth beyond news. This is where intuition comes in. It is the distillate of one's experiences and their interpretation. Often gut feel trumps market research. Our diversification into entertainment was wholly unplanned. The launch of our second channel had been wildly successful. In just 10 weeks CNN-IBN had equaled NDTV. We had acquired IBN7. That is when Viacom came to us looking for a partner. It had brands like Nickleodeon and MTV.

We had moved out of entertainment in the 1990s. We were producing serials. We did not own the rights. Without title to intellectual property, all we got was 10 percent pay off for our time and effort. Channels knew the cost of producing soaps. They did not leave much on the table. There was no way we could scale up this business. We decided to drop it.

Leadership for me is the ability to take contrarian calls. Early on, when my company was a chick breaking out of the shell, I decided to get out of the contract for India Business Report with BBC World. IBR was a weekly show, broadcast on Sundays. It was hugely popular. The platform on which it was broadcast, the journalistic values it embodied and the production quality gave us respectability. But it was a 10 percent production contract. Producing news shows for others would not let us rise up the food chain. We had to own the infrastructure of news for that—studios, outdoor broadcasting vans, and cameras. We gave up BBC World's job work, for a partnership with ABNi, a business news channel based in Singapore that had the *Wall Street Journal* and the Hindujas as parents.

But calamity stuck us not once but thrice. Even nature seemed to be against us. We had to conserve money and pay as we went. We had rented space underground. Once monsoon, rainwater flooded our basement office and studio. A few months later, a devastating fire gutted it. Luckily, no one was hurt. Without self-discipline one would have lost heart and become despondent. But we endured with fortitude. This is when an entrepreneur is called upon to draw on his inner reserves. We shifted to a pre-fabricated studio in Noida's Film City, when it was little more than fancy signboard. Some of my colleagues moved to Singapore and kept the show going. Their sense of ownership was touching.

I believe that for organizations to grow, they must let people perform. When you give them space, they develop a sense of ownership. This is not just a pecuniary thing, bought with high salaries and stock options. It is the psychic income that accrues from a feeling of belonging. That is when people say, "This is my work, I am responsible and I am going to do it the best I can." To me, it came from my father, when he took my "no" with grace to his suggestion that I attempt the civil services. It instilled in me an important leadership belief that if people are made to do something against their will, there will be temporary compliance. Achievement and excellence cannot be forced. Forced compliance is bad for a leader's standing. It harms the enterprise as well. People blossom when they do things of their own volition.

I have found that the ability to empower is critical to leadership. The corollary of empowerment is trust. Without trust, you will be second-guessing a person's sincerity all the time. Respect, trust, and empowerment are articles of faith with me. This is what has held my team together.

I also believe that a leader must be accessible. I must be one of the most accessible persons to my colleagues. At one time they could walk into my room anytime. They cannot do that now because I keep a tight schedule. But they can send me an email and expect a quick reply. For me, this is a cornerstone of leadership. I am sure this trait was born in me when my parents left me to decide for myself and even make mistakes. I made quite a few. But I was never hauled up for them. I was never forced to do anything against my wish. My parents were always around as mentors, as supporters. One has unconsciously imbibed their style.

I believe that leaders must celebrate mistakes. Quite a few of them do not. Without mistakes it is not possible to improve and progress. Those who are not making mistakes are playing safe. They are lacking in initiative. The moment you recognize and learn from mistakes, you have made the quantum jump to the next step. In my organization, people are not pulled up for honest mistakes. If they deliberately mess up, it is another story. There is a difference between mistakes and negligence.

As I said earlier, adversity is an entrepreneur's constant companion; the strength to overcome it is the true mark of leadership. Without the ability to "never say die", one can sink into despair. It can wreck an enterprise. It happened to us with ABNi. One year, around Christmastime when the East Asian countries were ravaged by the financial contagion, ABNi and CNBC announced a merger. The Tiger economies were faltering; there was just not enough advertising to support two business channels. The news came as a blow to us. We had hired a large number of people and invested in equipment. We had worked hard to be seen and heard. All of a sudden, we felt the ground slipping from underneath. Our lifeline had been cut. We were hurtling into uncertainty.

The ABNi fiasco taught us the dangers of going to bed with giant partners. We were a ₹40 million company. The Hindujas and *Wall Street Journal* were behemoths. The contracts they drew were marvels of legalese. We were completely defenseless. But our reputation as good, reliable partners saved us. Our partnership with ABNi ended, but another one opened up. CNBC closed its India bureau and chose us as a partner. But we no longer had the budget to keep our entire team. We had to let people go, which itself was a lesson in transition leadership.

A leader not only has to manage the present; they have to anticipate the future. Technology and consumer preferences change, sometimes very quickly. The fittest competitor in one environment can become a laggard in another. For us the Internet is the future. We have been investing in it from the beginning. We think that India is the US with a lag. Earlier, we used to trail the US trends by about 20 years, then 10 years; now it is probably 2 or 3 years. The game of catch-up will accelerate with iPad-ization.

We almost set up a newspaper. After the financial crisis of 2008, it is unlikely that we ever will. We think that news in the future, English news at least, will be consumed digitally on iPads and other smart handheld devices. 4G services will push up the speed of data transmission; one will be able to get live streaming television on the go. I see digital handheld devices dominating news consumption. In anticipation, we have launched firstpost. com. This is a website that creates it own content; it does not recycle news like the digital versions of broadsheets and magazines. I keep a tab on the US media trends. I think India will evolve very similarly to the US in consumption patterns. We take great care to avoid repeating the mistakes, which the US media companies did. They did not give digital much importance. Can you imagine that CNBC sold its digital franchise to MSN early in the last decade and then bought it back to relaunch cnbc.com?

Web content and services are becoming viable in India with increased access and usage. In the transaction space, bookmyshow.com sold ₹4,500 million worth of movie and music concert tickets in 2011–2012. Homeshop 18, a television and online shopping service, did ₹6,400 million in sales that year. In news, moneycontrol.com is making money. We have 26 million visitors across our digital properties. At Web18, all the Internet sites are profitable, except in.com, which is still in the investment phase. The rollout of 4G broadband, and availability of cheaper smart handsets, will create massive network economies. We have shown technology and trend leadership.

In addition to taking predictive calls in new media technology, we have taken contrarian positions on traditional media. Though print media is still growing in India, we believe that it has just five to seven years of growth left. The print media is plateauing. We have decided to stay away from it.

To build or buy is a decision one has to often make. As a first-gen entrepreneur in a fast evolving industry, I have had to balance between developing own businesses and acquiring them. We brought moneycontrol.com, Viacom18, IBN7, and Eenadu. We built IBN, in.com, and Colors. Many large media houses are unable to take such bets because they are busy protecting their empires against intrepid, devil-may-care guys like us.

Entrepreneurs are driven by a high need for achievement. They want to perpetuate what they have created. Legacy is intrinsic to enterprise. I was 35 years old when I pioneered business television news in India. I could have remained a boutique player. But I told myself that I could do much more with the 25 or 30 years I had. We now have size. I would like to convert these into market strength and profitability. By the time I hang up my boots, I would like to leave behind a huge Indian media operation like Time Warner or Walt Disney.

Chapter 7

Leadership: A Personal Narrative

—Tarun Das

This is a personal narrative, but for a person who worked in and for a public, national institution for 46 years, it is difficult to use the word "I." Many people played a part in my success in ways that the "I" seems very much out of place.

And, it was sheer luck that this career opened up and happened. My father had heard of a possible opening at the Bengal Chamber of Commerce during my job-hunting days after university in 1963. I started off as a management trainee with a lump-sum salary of ₹750 per month.

The work was interesting, challenging, involving multi-skilling. A hard British boss was a taskmaster extraordinaire, and the rest is history.

Introduction

Thoughts of a higher aspiration came from an early realization, in the 1970s, that an industry institution or business association could do more than just work for incentives or concessions, which was the traditional role of an industry organization at the time.

Those were tough times, with the government micro-managing the economy and industry. All industrial activity was controlled, be it investment, expansion, diversification, export, import, etc. So, at one level, the drive was to deal with hurdles and bottlenecks and, at another, to seek a new path of industrial development.

That an institution of industry could really make a difference flowed from the then-unthinkable merger of the Indian Engineering Association (IEA) and the Engineering Association of India (EAI) in April 1974 in Calcutta (now Kolkata). The IEA was affiliated to ASSOCHAM and Bengal Chamber, the EAI to Federation of Indian Chambers of Commerce and Industry (FICCI) and the Indian Chamber.

The merger agreement provided for an association which would not be affiliated to either of the apex chambers of commerce (unprecedented at that time), would relocate its headquarters to Delhi and would work differently (yet to be defined) and be data-based in its representations and interaction with the government.

Another major idea was that the association would do things and work in areas where government assistance was not a pre-requisite. One manifestation of this was the organizing of the first-ever Indian Engineering Trade Fair (IETF) in February 1975 at very short notice. It was an industry initiative to project Indian engineering industry capability. And, this was done at a time of national debate and crisis leading to the Emergency later in 1975.

The merger and the Trade Fair gave a new feeling of faith and confidence of doing things differently, contributing to change on a wider canvas, in fact, a national canvas, and this, then, flowed back to the members, office-bearers, and staff of the association.

There was a "big picture" scenario of playing a pioneering role, breaking new ground, and bringing about change for the better. The staff was highly motivated to stretch, to work 24*7, to try new ideas and activities, programs and projects.

But, 1974–1984, the first 10 years in New Delhi were difficult times: of struggle and hard work, of shortage of financial resources, of limited number of staff, of an unknown "brand" and a national environment of the Emergency, two general elections, changes in government and, finally, the assassination of Prime Minister Indira Gandhi on October 31, 1984.

Throughout this period, the organization continued to chart its path, however challenging. Trade fairs continued. Overseas missions were mounted. Overseas offices were opened—this, too, was unprecedented for an industry association. And—on the policy front, public articulation of the need to free the economy, free trade and investment, free imports of technology, allow competition, and accept the pain to restructure.

The organization, though relatively small, became known for leadership, as a change agent and for new initiatives.

In 1984–1985, it ventured into the beginning of a new international partnership with the World Economic Forum (WEF), which became its bridge to the world through Davos and the annual India Economic Summit in Delhi.

This was another new dimension—the commitment to connect India to the world to India in spite of the fact that India was still "closed."

The organization belief, in itself, to bring about change never faltered and, gradually, industry rallied around carrying the flag of liberalization, often not fully understanding the implications.

The executive team was excited, enthusiastic, and energetic, pushing new ideas, creating new initiatives, motivating themselves and the association membership.

Rajiv Gandhi as prime minister reinforced this. He encouraged the association, brought new ideas to the country, and became a force for change. Connecting India to the world—visiting USA and China, for example—-were huge initiatives taken by him. Developing technology in India in the face of technology denials was his driver for S&T. Liberalizing the economy, opening it to competition, and driving the quality movement was another direction set by him. Using information technology and the computer to change India was another huge initiative.

The years 1984–1989 became a time of change and new excitement, which was completely in tune with the Association of Indian Engineering Industry (AIEI) (Confederation of Engineering Industry [CEI] was the new name in 1986) ethos and culture. It became a period of national recognition for AIEI/CEI, and the motivated team in the institution started seeing the rewards of doing things differently after 10 years of struggle.

All this strengthened this institution enormously, and the foundations set in 1974, the conventions adopted then, continued to guide the organization. The amazing thing was the synergy between office-bearers and the staff who worked as one team without artificial or any other barriers of the employer–employee equation.

Vision

There was no big vision to begin with. The focus was on creating a new kind of institution, moving away from past legacies, putting together an executive team which would be ready to run and stretch, getting away from bureaucracy, red-tape, and procedures which hampered work.

The vision came later through trying new activities and initiatives and seeing that each one was a success. Building blocks of success—trade fairs, missions, exhibitions overseas, overseas offices, participating in Davos, organizing the India Economic Summit with WEF, etc.—continued and each one fell into place and all together became a canvas of growth and achievement.

In addition, the policy of working in partnership with the government, not in confrontation, but by building trust and cooperation began, together bringing change in India, for India, and for Indian industry. Governments responded warmly to this reaching out for a team approach.

Gradually, the vision developed:

- To build an institution for change and development, going beyond past traditions
- Being the projector of Indian industry, its technology, and capability
- Being the presenter of confidence and the driver for change
- Being the bridge to the world and bringing the world to India
- Driving for policy liberalization, a freer economy, and openness not witnessed since 1947 and Independence

These multiple visions were not in watertight compartments. These were interconnected, overlapping, moving concurrently to build a newer India. That the association was in a way playing a central role, was enormously exciting to everyone—staff and volunteer office-bearers.

The years 1984–1989 saw the vision being formulated and framed.

The years 1991–1996 saw the vision consolidated and executed.

Year 1991 was also the year the organization was renamed Confederation of Indian Industry (CII) after years of internal debate, reflecting its wider charter and the decision to build a larger role for itself.

The name change to CII placed a new, huge responsibility, and a new race started to make sure that the name change was reflected in its activities, membership, and services.

The excitement grew. The adrenaline flowed. The energy flowed. The CII exploded with growth.

THE REALIZATION DAWNED THAT:

- An institution is much more than an individual or a company.
- An institution is for public service.
- An institution has a wide and long reach.
- An institution belongs to many.
- An institution can bring about change.
- An institution is for development.
- An institution is accountable to the public.

Organizational Growth

A very critical issue was to frame a solid constitution but, even more important, to write out a set of "Conventions" to be followed. These were the "spirit" of the organization. For example, "no canvassing for elections." Or, "office-bearers term was strictly for one year." Or, office-bearers would not use their office for their company work. These were amazingly new concepts for an association of industry. And, these were real. Actually practiced and implemented.

The other facet was to build an "Independent" secretariat, a "professional" team—not bag carriers for bosses but performers and achievers in their own right, people who had ideas and the ability to execute and implement ("Doers").

This Secretariat became an amazing force in driving the association forward and earned applause from office bearers, membership, government, international bodies, media, etc. It provided continuity, it showed commitment, and it lit new fires.

And, yet, the respect for the National Council, the President and other office-bearers, the teamwork, was deep and abiding, reflecting mutuality and trust. The public profile was with office-bearers. The inner driving force was the staff team.

Very early in the day, in the 1970s and 1980s, it became clear that India and the Indian industry could not be serviced from only four cities, four offices. As part of strengthening and deepening the organization and its impact, the process began of setting up state offices and, even "zonal" offices in key cities like Pune, Coimbatore, Jamshedpur, etc.

The idea was to spread wings to be both national and local, to connect the dots, to be known by the same name everywhere, to build a common brand—a single brand—and, to have a network across the nation.

Concurrently, there was the plan to build an international outreach through overseas offices in key locations: London, Washington D.C., Singapore, Shanghai, Bonn, Paris, Melbourne, Tokyo, etc. This was supplemented with regular delegation visits, both ways, and Memoranda of Understandings (MoUs) with national industry organizations abroad and building an international partnership framework.

Even before the merger in 1974, it was clear that the Engineering Industry was not homogeneous. It was diverse. With growth this became even more evident. To deal with sector issues, the practice of industry divisions and sector committees was established so that service and support was extended to different industry sectors. As a result, a complex organization evolved.

National, regional, state, zonal, sectoral, subject-wise committees, overseas offices—there was no parallel in the world, never mind India. The growing secretariat reflected this expansion and complexity.

A very important fact was financial policy. The subscription rate was not changed for many years since there were numerous small firms as members. The policy and focus was to earn revenue through special services and activity, for example, TQM, Energy Conservation, Trade Fairs, etc. This was completely different from other similar organizations, which were largely subscription-dependent. This meant that the association staff had to be constantly alert, proactive, and competitive to earn their way to growth.

Another critical issue was the composition of staff. Trained, experienced staff was rare. So, the focus was on recruitment of young people and training them on the job, giving them trust and space to perform and supporting them through this process. Young people delivered incredibly well. They brought a quality of dynamism and energy quite unprecedented.

A sub-headline of this story is the emergence of young women executives in all parts of the organization, leading activity within India and overseas. Women contributed enormously to the work of the institution, and this mix of men and women was a formula for success.

Human beings are only human and the usual competition, turf issues, etc., were a usual part of work and life. But, work continued and achievements flowed.

An important element was to keep an open-door policy, to listen, to try to solve problems quickly, to avoid being bureaucratic, to be informal, and always remain connected with staff at all levels. This created a great work atmosphere for high productivity.

And, the team was always seeking to do things differently from other bodies. One was to view issues in the longer term; the second was to package activities differently; the third was to sustain programs beyond the ad hoc and the one-off.

So, if something new worked, do it again. For example, "Made in India" shows abroad. Once successful, became a model for other countries, especially in the developing world such as South Asia, Africa, and South-East Asia.

Some of the key criteria were to take initiatives, take leadership, take risk, bring about change for the better, and project India.

Organization growth followed rather than preceded, and this ensured minimal bureaucracy. There was central leadership and coordination, but there was also considerable space and freedom for different people to provide leadership in their areas of responsibility.

When the organization grew huge, there was need to review and restructure. External consultants were invited in and this, also, was a process which started in 1998 and went on till 2004. It re-sharpened vision, ideas, objectives, teamwork, etc.

Succession

It is the National Council or, actually, the president, vice president and past presidents who decide succession.

The outgoing chief executive does a couple of things.

He tries to ensure that there is talent within the organization. That automatically happened with growth and success. In fact, the organization was rich in very competent executives. And, this is proved by the subsequent leadership roles being performed by erstwhile CII executives in the corporate sector and institutions of repute.

The second is to give an impartial assessment of, say, the top 10 executives to the president. This was done based on 20+ criteria which are important in a leader. In fact, this assessment was requested by the then president of CII for his use and reference.

Eventually, the office-bearers decide, and they decided. They went over many possibilities—internal and external—and focused on seniority, maturity, and experience.

The internal dynamics within the presidents group are not known.

The future is very much dependent on sustained quality of leadership plus retention of talent. Exodus of talent can be a huge challenge for the institution which, then, is faced with an uphill, turnaround task of inducting fresh talent. But, perhaps this, too, is inevitable.

The institute having become very strong and successful can survive downturns. In the life of an individual or institution, ups and downs are inevitable and unavoidable. Reasons for this can be external and/or internal. But, a strong institution has the resilience to overcome.

Introspection is a very important part of the process, and in that, honesty of analysis and facing the facts is crucial. Papering over the truth is the worst. And, the process is always long term. There are no short cuts.

Some Components of Leadership

Leadership is integrity.
Leadership is listening to people.
Leadership is giving trust and space to staff and motivating them.
Leadership is the ability to take risk.
Leadership is the willingness to fail and learning from it.
Leadership is understanding that it's not a 100 meter race; it's a marathon.
Leadership is accepting success as a gift and not getting arrogant or complacent.

Leadership is believing that someone up there is looking after all of us.

Leadership is humility, modesty, and being understated.

Leadership is trying to minimize biases and prejudices.

Leadership is respecting women for their capability and potential.

Leadership is common sense.

Leadership Advice

Advice is cheap. Not really effective. Personal learning is the only way. Children do not listen to parents and prefer to make their own mistakes. The same applies to leaders of organizations. In fact, there is resistance and reluctance to learn from predecessors, never mind, elders. The best learning, therefore, is self-learning and, critically, learning from failures. There is very little learning from success.

Each leader wants to do it his or her way. This is the natural process. This is the way it is and will always be. And, therefore, failure is an inevitable part of leadership experience. Leadership development becomes stronger in this way.

Some simple issues are: listen; others before self; it's not about money only; be decisive; be honest; beware of ego; and the team is more important than the individual.

Chapter 8

Practicing Leadership in Contemporary India: A Personal Experience

—Chanda Kochhar

Introduction

I have always believed that leadership is not about theory, but about practice. It is not only about vision, but as much about execution. It is not just about having strategies or approaches set in stone, but about being adaptable and flexible. It is not about aggression, but about dynamism combined with prudence. And, most importantly, it is about learning—about seizing every opportunity, every challenge as an opportunity to learn and grow.

Over the last two decades, India has offered a tremendous canvas for leadership, and continues to do so. The fundamental economic changes have necessitated reinvention and also created new opportunities. There can be no better learning ground for leadership.

ICICI—earlier known as the Industrial Credit and Investment Corporation of India Limited—has been a major financial institution with deep moorings in the Indian economy since its inception in 1955. I joined the organization as a management trainee in 1984. Since then, I have been a part of the organization's ever-evolving strategy, and have risen through the ranks by handling multidimensional assignments, creating and running different businesses, and heading major functions at various points in time. It was not always easy. The constant challenge for me has been to evolve and adapt as the country and the organization transformed. Challenges spurred me to stretch beyond the familiar and the comfortable, look for opportunities of growth, and take on even bigger challenges. It meant completely reinventing myself as I went through this unique experience of running almost all areas of banking—project finance, commercial banking, retail banking, international banking, and corporate functions.

The final decade of the last century had unleashed unprecedented competitive pressures on the Indian economy, fueled by the twin forces of economic deregulation and technology. These forces shaped vast changes in the financial services sector, creating an era of discontinuous change and offering exciting prospects as well as hitherto unknown risks for the industry. These changes provided great opportunities for us to evolve new competencies to meet the changing dynamics of the new environment and enter new, uncharted areas of financial services.

The Retail Challenge

Consumer credit barely existed in India in the 1990s. Retail lending was under-penetrated, dominated by multinational banks which limited themselves to the niche consumer segment of affluent households. ICICI, till then essentially a project finance company with no presence in the consumer segment, decided to enter the retail credit segment in 1998, and I was asked to build this business shortly thereafter. The mandate was to create a consumer credit market, an area that was nascent in the country and completely unknown not only to the organization but also to me. While seeking to diversify our lending business into retail, we were also building the deposit franchise at ICICI Bank, which did not have the conventional infrastructure required for retail banking in the form of branches.

This was also the period when India was witnessing deep structural reforms. Strong economic growth, a favorable demographic profile and rising income levels were whetting the aspirations of a growing middle class and spurring consumption demand in the economy. Technology and the advent of the World Wide Web were changing business paradigms across the globe. The challenge was to think beyond the boundaries of existing business, recognize the under-penetration of retail lending and the importance of this segment in the context of the changing dynamics of India's growing consuming class and its aspirations. We proactively identified the key growth opportunity for the future ahead of the competition.

For me personally, this meant moving out of the Major Clients Group, which I was heading and which accounted for a substantial portion of ICICI's business and profits, and adapting again to a completely new environment. It meant moving out of my comfort zone and getting into uncharted territory. There was no roadmap to follow and no statistics to guide us into making the correct decision. In the absence of any markers on this journey, the key challenge was to find the right way to approach the market and arrive at every decision based on gut feel. For instance, we took a call to set up 3,000 ATMs over two years at a time when India had only 200–300-odd ATMs.

We knew that the only way to make a mark in consumer banking business was to attain scale. I had to capitalize on the opportunity for sustainable growth created by rising household incomes and the increasing awareness of retail financial services among consumers, with the aim of becoming the number one player in the business within three or four years. We positioned ICICI as a pan-India provider of a full suite of retail products, and made enhanced customer convenience our key selling proposition. We focused on delivering multiple products through multiple channels (branches, ATMs, Internet, and call centers), leveraged our strong corporate relationships to expand the range of business, focused on cross-selling and superior service quality at optimal cost. We opted for a technology-driven distribution model to provide greater convenience and flexibility to the rapidly growing discerning consumer and created a new paradigm in consumer credit distribution through doorstep and point-of-sale delivery. Soon, ICICI Bank was delivering modern banking services to millions of people, and offering them a wide range of products and services.

The other strategic challenge was creating a team. As it was a new business for us, I had to create a team of people who had worked in this industry for other banks. What I brought to that team was ICICI's strategic thinking, but when it came to domain knowledge or product nuances, I had to learn from the team. I was a leadership bridge between ICICI's way of thinking on the one hand and the domain knowledge of the team on the other hand. I had to arrive at decisions not based on past experience, but on a mix of their domain knowledge and my gut feel.

As it turned out, the retail sector grew by more than 50 percent per annum, year-on-year, for many years. In five years, ICICI Bank was one of the largest players in the consumer credit business in India. Indeed, in the process of transforming a small bank into the largest private sector bank in the country, within a decade of its inception, the various steps we took shaped the retail finance industry in India.

Moving on: CFO and CEO

If the retail challenge was to enter a completely unexplored area, the challenge that I faced in 2009 was to rework the growth strategy and lead the organization through a critical period of rapid change in global financial landscape. The speed with which the global financial crisis impacted the world was unanticipated. The events of 2008 revealed the increasingly complex nature of business, and the fact that business leaders needed to be constantly aware of the speed of change and be agile and quick to react to different situations while planning their strategies. It also highlighted the need to constantly reassess the market environment and plan for long-term growth, even if it resulted in a period of adjustment over the short term. The challenges and the rapidity of their emergence created a mood of shock and erosion of confidence among business, consumers, and investors. ICICI Bank had enjoyed a period of unprecedented high growth for several years, and the challenge that I faced was to realign the organization's strategy to the new environment, shift gear from growth to consolidation and get the team accustomed to high growth, to buy into the vision and execute it well. It was a completely new template. The five-year strategy started with a significant shift of gear from growth to consolidation in the initial phase. Even though this strategy resulted in moderation in business volumes in the initial period, it placed us in a better position to participate in the renewed growth cycle. In the first stage of this strategy, we repositioned the balance sheet for the next phase of growth. In fiscal 2010, we focused on rebalancing the asset liability mix, improving cost efficiency, and reducing credit costs while maintaining a strong capital position. In fiscal 2011, we moved to the next stage to resume growth by capitalizing on the emerging opportunities in the Indian economy, while maintaining and enhancing the more efficient balance sheet structure achieved in fiscal 2010. This resulted in a robust growth in the Bank's loan portfolio with improved profitability.

Leadership Lessons

I treated challenges as opportunities not just to learn for my own development but also to create something new for the organization. I could bring in synergy when I moved from corporate to consumer banking, and deep insights from India that could be implemented globally when I moved from consumer banking to international banking. The supervisory roles enabled me to appreciate the challenges of a business in a rational way. Indeed, I evaluate a leader more in terms of how the leader performs in difficult times, rather than how he or she performs in a buoyant marketplace. One has to always aim to convert challenges into opportunities. A person who can take on a challenge and maintain equanimity and turn it into an opportunity is the best leader.

It is also my firm belief that a leader needs to be adaptable so that he or she can quickly understand and move forward in new business situations. It is the environment that should take precedence and drive the organization in any strategy formation. Indeed, the main tenet of a successful business leader is the ability to respond continuously to a complex, unpredictable environment calling for unconventional decisions under ambiguous conditions. The ability of the leader to foresee change and prepare the organization for the coming environment rather than just coping with the existing environment is very important to the success of an organization. Indeed, the experience of the post-Lehman world reinforced in me the criticality of the environment. My immediate priority was to reassess the market environment and realign the strategy of ICICI Bank to the new economic environment. Following the global financial crisis, the economic growth outlook was reduced sharply even for countries with strong domestic drivers, like India, and predictions of a severe downturn became common. We decided to embrace caution, move into a consolidation phase, and reposition the balance sheet for the next phase of growth.

Strategies can only be implemented in an organization's cultural context. A leader needs to ensure that the organization's innovation, energy, and competitiveness are never lost. The DNA of ICICI Bank and quality of our workforce and their dynamism have also been a key factor in our success. ICICI Bank's ability as an organization to be adaptable, flexible, and responsive to the needs of the emerging business environment and the ability of the team to execute a strategy with speed and accuracy provided me with the necessary ammunition to implement change successfully. ICICI Bank believes in empowerment, innovation, and the fact that there is nothing that it cannot achieve as a team. This, combined with ethics and good governance, has been the Bank's biggest strength and which has given us a strong foundation, as well as the ability to change course when required. These strong traditions and deeply held beliefs aided the Bank in the past and also helped us to lead the charge in the second phase. It helped me execute a growth strategy when the environment demanded that strategy and a consolidation strategy when the environment demanded one.

The last two years have proved that it is imperative to put every strategy in proper perspective and articulate it very clearly to ensure that it is implemented. One cannot simply issue a new strategy and expect compliance. To successfully implement any change in strategy, there is a need to build an understanding of the organization's position and strategy within its customers, investors, regulators, and employees. Throughout 2009 and 2010, we stressed on the importance of clear communication. We undertook a multipronged program, and I spent a large portion of my time explaining the relevance of the new strategy to employees, investors, and regulators. We demonstrated steady progress to regulators and investors. I made it a point to respond to each and every piece of mail that came to me. We also needed to convince employees, so accustomed to a period of very aggressive growth, of the overall need for the change. I visited branches, met employees, listened to their concerns, and explained the challenge and need for the solution. This helped me be in close touch with the ground reality. We blended the discipline of meeting financial targets with a vision of how these steps would enable ICICI Bank to resume growth down the road. A mix of short-term realism and long-term idealism gave employees the right combination of push and pull, allowing them to persevere through the consolidation and look to the future. Indeed, all these steps did help in building confidence among stakeholders in the background of a volatile operating environment and ensured stability of the overall system.

Looking Ahead

As I look toward the future, I see many opportunities. The Indian economy has entered a phase where domestic consumption and investments—the two drivers of growth—will shape the economy and provide the foundation for growth. The strong fundamental factors of domestic demand and global competitiveness will continue to drive sustained growth in the foreseeable future. India will be one of the key drivers of global growth; the turmoil in Western economies and the relative insulation of Asia have only heightened this trend. Although periodic challenges will continue on account of global developments, volatility in capital flows, inflation and other factors, we see strong fundamentals driving sustained high growth in India. We will witness a virtuous cycle of growth which should propel us to a high growth trajectory and then sustain it for the next 15–20 years.

Economic growth and investment in infrastructure will drive urban development and urban rejuvenation. This will take many forms—modernization and redevelopment of existing large cities, expansion and upgradation of existing second-tier cities that are emerging as important engines of growth, and the creation of new towns in corridors of infrastructure development and industrial investment. The demographic shifts in terms of income levels and cultural shifts in terms of lifestyle aspirations will change the profile of the Indian consumer. Consumers will increasingly demand enhanced institutional capabilities and service levels from banks. Smaller markets beyond the large urban centers will emerge as important drivers of growth. Customer segments that were earlier nascent are maturing, and new customer segments have emerged. These distinct customer segments, with widely different requirements and risk-reward characteristics will require specialized strategies. This will call for aligning product development, customer acquisition, and customer servicing to the needs of specific customer segments. We will, therefore, continue to innovate and offer new services that will make financial transactions faster, simpler, and more secure, many of which will be the first of their kind in the industry.

At the same time, we will focus on the continuing challenge of inclusive growth. The engagement of a much larger section of our population in the economic mainstream through financial inclusion will be a key feature of our growth going forward. We have to understand the varying needs of rural customers, overcome barriers of distance, and solve the problem of the high cost-to-serve due to ticket sizes which are much lower than urban areas. Developments in low-cost information and communication technology and the unique identity (UID) initiative have the potential to rapidly accelerate financial inclusion by reducing the cost of providing access to basic financial services. The next step will be to expand access to financial services—savings, credit, insurance and payments services—to the underserved segments of society. The Bank is executing a focused financial inclusion plan leveraging information and communications technology and the enabling regulatory framework to provide basic banking services to the unbanked. At the same time, the importance of maintaining the social responsibility of businesses, that is, the voluntary consideration of public social goals apart from private economic ones, will remain an important facet in our outlook. Our vision encompasses not only participating in all aspects of the Indian economy and its international linkages, but also catalyzing India's growth. Through the ICICI Foundation for Inclusive Growth, we will seek to improve the quality of school education and primary healthcare in a number of states, thereby, playing its role in the strengthening of the soft infrastructure that is so critical to long-term sustainable growth of our country.

The momentum in the financial services sector has been driven to a significant extent by technology, and this would continue to be a key driver. The economic climate would continue to call for innovation, and technology will be used as a tool to accelerate the penetration of financial services. Indeed, the next game changer in banking and financial services will be biometric and communications technology. Biometric technology will change the way customers access financial services—the thumb would become the customer's passport into the financial world. The combination of biometric technology for authentication, wireless communications technology for carrying out transactions and maintaining seamless records at both the service provider end and the customer end, will rapidly accelerate financial inclusion, transform the customer's engagement with the financial system, and enhance the efficiency of the financial system.

Of course, this growth, these opportunities will bring their own set of leadership challenges as well. The pace of change in the

21st century is going to be even faster than it has been in the past. The ability of the leader to foresee change and prepare the organization for the coming environment, rather than just coping with the existing environment, will be very important for the success of an organization. Our capacity to adapt ourselves to the changing dynamics of market and consumer behavior and yet preserve the basic cultural anchors of our organization will, therefore, be central to our success as we go forward. I will continue to be inspired by what the Mahatma had once said, "any great organization, any great nation, any great entity has to be like a banyan tree with very strong roots but flexible branches," so that when the strong wind blows, the roots are firmly embedded in the ground and the branches sway with the tree and do not break.

In addition, what would be especially relevant for India is that as we keep growing at this fast pace, we have to rely on leadership that will be younger and younger. We are a young country. The pace of growth is actually faster than the rate at which our leadership is aging. As leaders, we will have to learn how to rely on younger and younger people: give them more responsibilities at a younger age, mentor them that much better, guide them that much more, and get them to handle more responsibilities. A substantial amount of my time will, therefore, be spent with my young leaders because every interaction with them will be an opportunity to groom them, an opportunity to make them buy into the vision that we have for the organization, and an opportunity to give them the comfort that the leadership will always be with them. In my interactions, I will look for entrepreneurial instinct in my young employees, as we have always believed that if you have to be a leader in building business, you will have to be an entrepreneur, open to lateral thought and decision-making. At the same time, I will also be looking at those who have the ability to manage multiple objectives at the same time, such as balancing growth and profitability and who are able to maintain balance while handling difficult situations.

In summary, leadership is best learnt experientially, by taking on challenges and seeking out opportunities. India is an exciting place to build and lead businesses, and will continue to be so given the growth dynamics of our country. The leaders who succeed will be those who combine forward-looking vision with a close connect with ground realities, balance growth with prudence, and empowerment with mentoring to create high-performing teams that build sustainable franchises.

Chapter 9

Leading Institutions and Thought Leadership

—R. A. Mashelkar

A Snapshot

I have been privileged to do science in India and also lead science in India. It was a pleasant surprise and a rare honor to receive the JRD Tata Corporate Leadership Award in 1998. A surprise, because the award is not for science leadership but for corporate leadership. An honor, because the individual who received this award just before me in 1997 was Narayana Murthy, and the one who received it in 1999 was Azim Premji. It was an honor to be sandwiched between these two icons!

All my life I have worked in the Indian national laboratory system. During the time, I led National Chemical Laboratory (NCL) (1989–1995); it transformed itself into an International Chemical Laboratory. It did the seemingly impossible—exporting knowledge from an Indian laboratory to leading multinational companies. This was a first in Indian history. NCL had secured zero US patents in its entire history. From that, to become a leader in US patents in a span of just a decade was remarkable. I then led (1995–2006) the Council of Scientific and Industrial Research (CSIR) as its director general. Leading CSIR was not an easy task. Poor science–business linkages, bureaucracy, unionization (yes, believe me, that too by scientists), no "Team CSIR" spirit, low budgets with low morale, all these were preventing CSIR from reaching its truly high potential, when I assumed its leadership. From this state of affairs, CSIR was transformed to a user-focused, performance-driven organization, and became a model for publicly funded R&D organizations. In what follows, I will provide a personal account of the leadership challenges and the lessons learnt during these transformations.

Leading Transformation of National Chemical Laboratory

I joined NCL as a scientist on November 15, 1976. I left an attractive faculty position abroad and returned to India in my early 30s on a salary of ₹2,100 per month. On June 1, 1989, I became the director of NCL, which already had a high reputation in chemical research.

The challenge was to convert NCL from a very good laboratory into a front ranking world class laboratory. In 1989, the Indian industry was protected by huge tariff barriers. Industry was in sellers' market. NCL scientists responded by essentially doing import substitution, because that was what the Indian industry demanded.

Context decides the content. It was clear to me that if NCL continued to operate in this context, the content of the NCL research agenda would be just copy, copy, and copy. There was no way NCL could have changed the "national context" in those pre-1991 days, which was all centered around import substitution. So I said NCL will change its "own context." NCL will become the International Chemical Laboratory by shifting its role from a seller of knowledge to Indian industry to a seller of knowledge to the whole world, even to the US and Europe. The very statement that "National Chemical Laboratory" will become an "International Chemical Laboratory" created an incredible aspiration, which, to me, is always the biggest driver of change. But here was the big challenge. Until 1989, that is, in 39 years of its existence, NCL had not been able to secure even one single patent in the US! How can a laboratory with such an abysmal record of US patenting even dream of being an exporter of its knowledge to USA? It looked impossible.

I challenged the laboratory by saying that there is no limit to human imagination, no limit to human achievement, excepting the limits we put on ourselves. In the import substitution era, we had put limits on our thinking. I said let us unshackle ourselves. Think boldly. Think ahead. Let's lead and not follow. NCL was charged with a new "yes, we can" spirit! NCL learnt to read patents, write patents, break patents as it went into this tough game. When NCL licensed its hydrodewaxing technology patents to the multinational company, Akzo, in Europe in 1990, it was a historical event, since this was the first time a reverse transfer of technology from an Indian national laboratory to an advanced nation had taken place. This was followed by the licensing of patents on an innovative new process for an engineering plastic to the US multinational giant, General Electric. This success created great awareness about the value and rewards of patenting amongst the NCL scientists. Within less than five years, NCL developed a big client list, which included the top few global leaders from around the world, from General Electric to DuPont and from Cargil to Polaroid. And there was no looking back even after I left as the director. Two of Procter & Gamble's very recent products in the market are based on NCL patents that it had recently licensed!

Achieving all this required a big cultural change at and by NCL. We said no more "publish or perish." The new driver was "patent, publish, and prosper." We said Indian ideas must generate wealth for our nation, not for other nations, as used to be the case then. We incentivized the scientists. On NCL's foundation day, we started giving a silver medal and a cash prize for anyone who had succeeded in acquiring a US patent. Initially, there were barely a couple of medal winners. But the number kept on swelling as the awareness grew. Finally the number became so large that NCL stopped giving this medal! After all, the purpose for which the initiative was started was fulfilled.

The feeling of becoming an International Chemical Laboratory was heady. NCL raised its global ambitions. It started exploring unchartered territories. A new aspiration that NCL should also be a global knowledge-based services provider emerged. In 1990, NCL saw an invitation for a global bid for a World Bank consultancy contract for reforms of some leading Chinese chemical research institutions. NCL had never participated in a global bid before. But we said, let our past not be a burden on our future. We participated in the bid. NCL had to compete with the formidable US players, Arthur D Little, Chem Systems and International Development Planners. NCL beat them and won the consultancy contract. Later on, NCL learnt from the Indian embassy in Beijing that it happened to be the first ever consultancy offered from China to India. Interestingly, it had to come from a national laboratory that had got into the good habit of making impossible possible!

All this journey was not easy. There were some fundamental mindset issues. We dealt with them by challenging ourselves. For instance, for all these years, NCL was used to getting government grants, no loans. NCL went out and got a World Bank loan. The good thing about the World Bank loan was that it had to be returned; not by the government, but by NCL itself! How could it be returned, if NCL did not create surpluses or profits? That meant doing research as a business. That was not easy. When I created a new Business Development Group in NCL, I came under attack from some leading scientists. They said Mashelkar is bringing the word "business" in the organization. That is going to corrupt the minds of the scientists. But none of that happened. NCL grew its business both qualitatively and quantitatively, and so was the case with its scientific research output with some breakthroughs in science appearing in leading journals at the same time. NCL showed that high science and science-based business could indeed coexist.

Leading CSIR Transformation

I led CSIR, a 20,000-strong family of 40 laboratories for a record of eleven and half years (1995–2006). the CSIR is the largest publicly funded industrial research and development chain of laboratories in the world. CSIR was born in 1942. CSIR went through different phases. In the 1950s, CSIR was trying to get some respectability for Indian science. The 1960s was the time when CSIR started addressing the challenge of applying science for the good of the Indian people. The era of indigenous technology development for the Indian industry started then. The 1970s was the time, when CSIR started learning the real intricacies of the journey from the mind to market place. The lessons that CSIR learnt gave it the confidence in the 1980s to become more adventurous. Like entering high-technology areas, such as modern bio-technology, advanced materials, etc. The 1990s was the time when CSIR said, "Why should we be beggars and borrowers of technology from the rest of the world? Should we not have the dream of exporting our knowledge to the outside world, especially the developed world?" So, a transformation started, where CSIR's client list expanded from Indian enterprises to global enterprises. In the ensuing years and beyond, an exciting thrust on excellence and relevance emerged; excellence in terms of being first to the world, whether in science or in technology. Relevance meant contributing to the national agenda of inclusive growth through science led inclusive innovation.

I was appointed the director general of CSIR on July 1, 1995. A month before I took the office, someone asked me about my dream for CSIR. I said, "CSIR incorporated." Then what was the dream for myself? I said, "Chief Executive Officer of CSIR." In fact, I remember a nice clipping in a newspaper referring to me as a corporate scientist, who thought the corporate way and talked the corporate language!

Within the first year of my taking over, I visited each of the 40 CSIR laboratories, which were spread from Kashmir to Kanyakumari. I addressed over 20,000 members of the CSIR family. I saw a big cultural divide between the CSIR institutions and the industry. The fact that science has to make an economic and social sense had not dawned on a large number of laboratories in CSIR, whereas demand on science from Indian industry was sadly missing. The CSIR laboratories worked on the basis of scientific novelties and perceived needs, whereas the business worked on the basis of attractiveness in the market and potential for profit. The products from the CSIR institutions invariably came out as packages containing knowledge and information, whereas the business was looking for only finished goods and services, which were saleable.

The main challenge was to see that industry viewed the CSIR laboratories as idea generators, providers of new concepts, and windows on knowledge on the rest of the world. I tried to persuade the Indian industry to assume the role of partners, who had the technical, financial, and marketing strengths to take the ideas to the market place. I tried to convince the industry that it should not look at the CSIR laboratories as super markets, where off the shelf technologies were sold, but in the true spirit of partnership, the Indian industry should willingly integrate CSIR R&D resources into their business strategy. I tried to create a climate of improved communication and understanding, faith in mutual growth, and development of healthy working relationships. But to build this trust and confidence in Indian industry, I had to show that CSIR itself was willing to change.

In January 1996, we released *CSIR 2001: Vision & Strategy*, a white paper, which was an announcement of CSIR's will to change. It was an explicit agenda for CSIR with a detailed road map for attaining the true potential of the organization. We defined a new product and a new process in CSIR. The new product was research as a business. The new process was doing research in a businesslike manner. We were enthused when the corporate world appreciated the vision paper. I remember Mr Ratan Tata, in a private conversation with me, called it a unique corporate like document from a publicly funded organization.

The *CSIR 2001 Vision* document was an important milestone. I brought this out after a wide consultation with our stakeholders, both internal as well as external. I remember Dr A. P. J. Abdul Kalam, our former president, was a member of the Advisory Board. He was a great friend and a guide for CSIR. When I spoke about

Vision 2001, he said, "Why don't you have Vision 2020?" I said, "I retire in 2002. I will like to be judged before I retire."

There was yet another challenge. CSIR had 40 laboratories, and they had always behaved like 40 separate laboratories. The sense of belonging to a family of CSIR was missing. Amazingly, that alignment began to happen with the creation of the vision document for CSIR 2001. So following CSIR 2001, came NCL 2001, CMRI 2001, CFRI 2001; all individual laboratories aligning themselves to the vision of CSIR 2001. The CSIR laboratories were like disoriented magnetic needles placed on a paper. It was like bringing a magnet near the paper, by which all these randomly placed needles started orienting and aligning by responding to the magnetic power of the CSIR 2001 vision!

My fulfilling moment was on May 11, 1998, when we had CSIR Directors' Conference in Bangalore. The theme of that conference was TEAM CSIR. I was deeply touched when in a charged closing ceremony, all the 40 directors spontaneously signed on a Bangalore declaration saying, "India matters to us. It is our endeavor that we shall matter to India, more." This was a perfect alignment of all the leaders to a common goal.

We made conscious efforts to ensure that the power was not centered in Delhi at the headquarters; it was where the action was. We, thus, empowered the directors in the laboratories allowing them freedom in decision-making. Autonomy goes with accountability. We built performance-based budget allocation systems for the laboratories. Each laboratory was asked to develop a business plan, not just a research plan. We set targets not only on the external

earnings but also on the new production to be catalyzed in industry, new jobs to be created, etc. The tangible impact of CSIR on
industry and society had to be assessed and measured not just for
CSIR's sake, but for the sake of the nation.

I kept on making a conscious effort to awaken the scientist in
an entrepreneur and an entrepreneur in a scientist. If a scientist
created wealth for the nation through the technologies developed
by him, then we felt that he should also get a share of this wealth.
So we created incentive schemes for these scientists, both at the
individual and institutional level. At an individual scientist level,
we said the salary does not have to be equal to the income. In
fact, the income can be much higher than the salary. We gave a
handsome share to the scientists from the royalties and licensing fees that were earned. At the institutional level, we allowed
the laboratories to build a corpus through the net surpluses that
they generated by offering their knowledge products to industry.
The laboratories were allowed full freedom to use the surpluses
in the way they wanted. This meant autonomy and freedom, but
only to the performers, who generated surpluses. No surplus, no
freedom! We allowed our laboratories to set up commercial arms.
The CSIR scientists were allowed to be on the boards of directors of both public sector and private sector companies. Similarly our Research Councils of all individual laboratories drew
up to 50 percent of its members from the corporate world. This
brought that much needed corporate culture and thinking in the
laboratories. We could see the visible difference that was brought
about when Subroto Ganguly of IPCL chaired the Research Council

of NCL or Jamshed Irani of (then) TISCO, chaired the Research Council of National Metallurgical Laboratory.

Progress through partnership at all levels—local, national, and global—was CSIR's goal. For this, we had to build strong internal knowledge networks within CSIR by building a TEAM CSIR spirit. We launched such major TEAM CSIR efforts in areas, where India could emerge as a global leader. For instance, India is described as a rich country, where poor people live. Our richness, among other things, is due to our rich biodiversity and our rich traditional medicinal systems. India had so far not been able to exploit this advantage. For this purpose, CSIR launched a program on discovery and development of bioactives based on plant and other sources by bringing traditional medicine, modern medicine and modern science together. Twenty of the CSIR laboratories were networked together in this exciting endeavor. Other similar networks followed. This was the first time in the history of CSIR that such massive networking and synergy were built.

Going further, while building strong linkages with the corporate world in India, CSIR built global partnerships by realizing that the chain of concept to commercialization necessarily crosses transnational boundaries. As a part of the global innovation strategy, several companies world over were scouting for new ideas and patents. Taking advantage of this strategic shift, CSIR forged global partnerships. Thus Mobil and Indian Institute of Petroleum (IIP) joined hands to jointly develop and market the Mobil–IIP technologies worldwide. Stone & Webster of the US partnered for implementing IIP's technologies on visbreaking. SmithKline

Beacham joined hands with Indian Institute of Chemical Technology (IICT) in some exciting projects on drugs. Boeing partnered with National Aerospace Laboratories (NAL) for some crucial fatigue research. NAL's software supplied to Civil Aviation Authority in the UK started determining the landing frequency of aircrafts at the Heathrow airport. NCL's partnerships with giants, such as General Electric, became a model for external R&D alliances. On March 4, 1995, I had delivered the Thapar Memorial Lecture. Dr Manmohan Singh, who was then the finance minister of India, chaired this lecture. It was titled "India's Emergence as a Global R&D Platform: The Challenges and Opportunities." No one had believed me then. But they believe it now. Today, over 760 companies from abroad have set up their R&D centers in India, from GE to GM, from IBM to CISCO, from Dow to DuPont, and from Nokia to Shell.

While CSIR was forging global corporate level partnerships, not for a moment did it forget its basic charter in terms of doing what was good for India. CSIR created jobs for the poor in India. Central Institute of Medicinal and Aromatic Plants (CIMAP) had a breakthrough on menthol mint, on which 70 percent of menthol production in India was based. More than five million man-days of jobs were created, essentially for the poor. India also displaced China to the second position as an exporting nation. CSIR breakthrough on the E-MAL, which is an anti-malaria drug for cerebral malaria, was another breakthrough. These affordable drugs were supplied not only to Indians, but to 48 countries in the world, many of them from sub-Saharan Africa. Central Leather Research

Institute (CLRI) was the savior of the Indian leather industry. CLRI brought back tanneries that were closed due to pollution by developing green technology. This saved several thousands of jobs for the underprivileged poor. CSIR demonstrated by action that India mattered to it, and it wanted to matter to India, more.

This CSIR transformation in the 1990s has been held as one of the top 10 achievements of Indian science and technology in the 20th century in the book titled as *Scientific Edge* by India's celebrated scientist, Jayant Narlikar. A cover story has been written by *Business India* on the CSIR transformation. It was the first time such a cover story on Indian science and technology appeared in any business magazine. A chapter on CSIR transformation appeared in a book titled *World Class in India* published by Penguin for management students. The book was all about how Indian entities managed radical change in the post-liberalized India. Among the editors of the book, was the global management guru, Sumantra Ghoshal. CSIR's case study featured along with the case studies for Reliance, Wipro, Infosys, etc. The World Bank has used the CSIR transformation as a model for institutional transformation. In fact, I remember Jim Wolfensohn, the president of the World Bank, inviting me to come to Moscow and share the experience of CSIR transformation with a presentation to the prime minister of Russia, so that Russian institutions could learn from the experience of CSIR transformation!

I received an invitation to speak about the CSIR transformation in the series "Ideas That Have Worked" set up by Mr Arun Shourie, when he was the minister in the Indian cabinet in the year 2000. In that series, Dr A. P. J. Abdul Kalam spoke about his Vision 2020.

Chandrababu Naidu spoke about converting Hyderabad into Cyberabad. M. S. Swaminathan spoke about the Green Revolution. Verghese Kurien spoke about the White Revolution. Ratan Tata spoke about the making of Indica. Mukesh Ambani spoke about the making of the giant Indian enterprise, Reliance. To rank CSIR transformation along with these epochal Indian achievements was something very special for me.

How do I look back on my leadership? John Adams had famously said, "If your actions inspire others to dream more, learn more, do more and become more, you are a leader."[1] I earnestly hope that when others judge my leadership, I will be able to clear this acid test of leadership at least with passing marks, if not with flying colors.

Thought Leadership

Thought and action are both important in leadership. The power of thoughts can transform nations, if the thoughts are converted into action. Such thought leadership, if pursued with passion and patience (yes, in India, one does require that), it can yield phenomenal results.

From my personal experience, I would like to highlight three areas: first, the thought that Indian ideas must be patented by Indians so that the wealth can be created in India. The second is the thought that the "I" in India must stand for innovation, and not

---

[1] Quote by the second US President, John Quincy Adams (1779–1801). Available at www.philosiblog.com.

imitation, and therefore, like a freedom movement, there should be an Indian innovation movement. And the third facet is that if the thoughts are powerful enough then the top political leadership owns them, champions them, and that can make a huge difference. Let us begin with my experience of the third facet first.

I had given a talk "Mind vs Mindset: The Grand Indian Challenge" on August 9, 2008, in Lucknow in an event organized by the All India Management Association (AIMA). I had then said,

> India has three things, which will stand for it in good stead. They all have to do with innovation and creativity because only those nations will survive and succeed in the 21st century which are great in innovation and creativity. So, what are those three things? They are three Ds: Democracy, Diversity, and Demography.

Our prime minister released the first report to the People of National Innovation Council on November 15, 2011. In his address, he said, "There are some advantages that we have in achieving the task that we have set for ourselves. Our democracy, our diversity and our demography are all facilitating factors which encourage innovation in our country."[2] It was so wonderful to see the prime minister himself championing these thoughts.

And here is yet another example of the thought leadership. The Government of India had created an oversight committee under the chairmanship of Veerappa Moily in the year 2005 to consider the implementation of the government's reservation policy in

[2] National Innovation Council. 2011. "Report to the People." New Delhi: Government of India.

the higher educational institutions (such as the Indian Institute of Technologies [IITs]). In my very first meeting with the chairman, I suggested to him a guiding principle for the committee. That was about balancing "expansion, inclusion, and excellence." He saw the merit in it immediately. I am very happy that the entire Moily committee report was built around this theme. The National Knowledge Commission report (2009) championed this thought further by stating that "converting India into a knowledge society shall require, inter alia, addressing the issue of *expansion, excellence and inclusion* in education."[3] The president of India, in her address to the Parliament on June 4, 2009, endorsed this thought too by emphasizing "Government's strategy for higher education will be formulated around a threefold objective of *expansion, inclusion and excellence.*"

But it is not the political leadership accepting the thoughts that matter. Action matters. And I will provide now examples, where thoughts and action went together. Our intellectual property rights (IPR) journey began in a small way in NCL, but then it spread to CSIR, which was a chain of 40 NCL like national laboratories. In 1996, CSIR was the first one to announce a formal institutional IPR policy in India. And the results started showing. The list of the top 50 patent filers under Patent Cooperations Treaty (PCT) used to be published annually by the World Intellectual Property Organization (WIPO) in Geneva. India hardly figured in this list.

[3] National Knowledge Commission. 2009. "National Knowledge Commission Report." New Delhi: Government of India.

But then there came a time, when CSIR rose to the number one position, even ahead of companies like Samsung and LG. CSIR, for quite a while, held the leadership position with almost half to two-thirds of the share of US patents granted to India.

And as the IPR message spread; it attracted the attention of national leaders in science, technology, and business. Let me give just two examples. In the early 1990s, Dr A. P. J. Abdul Kalam was heading the Defence Research and Development Organization (DRDO). He asked me to address the directors of DRDO in a meeting that was held in Pune. I gave a hard talk about the need for the research laboratories to be patent literate. In an after-lunch conversation, I remember Dr Kalam saying to me, in all his characteristic humility that he did not know enough about patents. And he asked me as to what role patenting would play in DRDO. I explained to him the difference that patents could make to DRDO. Dr Kalam was a highly action-oriented man. I remember his immediately calling some senior DRDO scientists and asking them to introduce systems on IPR protection in the DRDO on the lines of CSIR. And today, DRDO is doing so well in protecting its own IPR.

The power of this thought went beyond the government-funded institutions. In the mid-1990s, I remember an air journey from Jamshedpur to Pune with Dr Jamshed Irani, who was then the managing director of TISCO, which is now Tata Steel. He wondered about the importance of patenting in steel industry, which was, after all, such a mature industry. I convinced him about the role of patenting even in steel industry. And then I remember Dr Irani requesting me to send the head of the Intellectual Property Management

Division of CSIR to interact with the TISCO R&D staff. Dr Irani then galvanized his people to an extent that Tata Steel has become a frontrunner in IP creation and protection in the steel industry now.

And this thought leadership on intellectual property influenced the Indian intellectual property policies too. By January 1, 2005, India had to meet an international obligation. It had to introduce the changes in the IPR legislation to make the Indian laws compatible with TRIPS, that is, Trade Related Aspects of Intellectual Property Rights. But this had to be done while ensuring that Indian interests were fully protected. I remember my intense involvement in this national challenge.

Pubic awakening across the length and the breadth of India was very important, so complex were the issues and so important were the consequences of the changes. The Department of Industrial Policy and Promotion of the Ministry of Industry and Commerce held around 20–25 public meetings across the country, inviting 200–300 participants in each of these meetings from all walks of life. This series of meetings of public awakening began in New Delhi with a one-hour opening talk by me. Again, I repeated my message in the JRD Tata Corporate Leadership Award Lecture (1998) there. I said, "Erase the impression of India as a country that is ducking and avoiding to one where it is willing to aggressively face the global competition by leading with a positive intellectual property policy." It went so well that there was a demand that this lecture be repeated in all the remaining meetings across India! Well, I could not have done this physically by moving to 20–25 locations in India! So Rajeev Ratan Shah, who was then the secretary, made an innovative suggestion. His idea was to make a 30-minute video of my address on the need to change and play it in all those nationwide meetings. I would like to believe that at least in some small way, this influenced the national thinking. And I was so happy when the Patent Amendments Bill was finally passed by the Parliament.

Let me move to a second powerful thought. "Innovation" has become a buzz word now. But the title of my JRD Tata Corporate Leadership award lecture way back in 1998 was "On launching a National Innovation Movement." I had proposed,

> Finally, 1999 should be the year, where we should launch a powerful national innovation movement to propel us into the next millennium. The "I" in India, should not stand for imitation and inhibition, it must stand for innovation. The "I" in every individual Indian must stand for innovation. It is only this innovative India that will signal to the rest of the world, that we are not a hesitant nation, unsure of our place in the new global order, but a confident one, that is raring to go and be a leader in the comity of nations.

Again I repeated this message in the January 2000 in my Science Congress Presidential address, when I proposed the New Panchsheel for the New Millennium, a five-point national agenda, which comprised child-centered India, woman-centered family, human-centered development, knowledge-centered society, and innovation-centered India. And yet again, speaking during the lecture series "Ideas That Have Worked" in New Delhi in April

2000, I repeated the message in the JRD Tata lecture practically verbatim. And I kept on repeating it persistently and relentlessly throughout the nation for almost a decade and almost month after month!

I was delighted when the prime minister, in his inaugural speech at the Science Congress in 2010, formally declared the decade 2010–2020 as the Indian Decade of Innovation. And I was further delighted, when this announcement was followed by the formation of Prime Minister's National Innovation Council under the leadership of one of India's most visionary innovation leaders, Sam Pitroda. And I was even more delighted when the idea of an Indian inclusive innovation fund at a national level (that was proposed by me) was accepted and the Indian Inclusive Innovation Fund was formally announced by the then Finance Minister Pranab Mukherjee on November 15, 2011, in New Delhi in the presence of the prime minister.

And here is a final thought on thought leadership. As reflected earlier, it is true that great thoughts and great action must go together. But thought leadership is an essential part of great leadership. Thought leaders look at the future. They are often ahead of their time. They set a courageous course that others are compelled to follow, sooner or later. True thought leaders think of the "next practices"—not just the "best practices." They ferment a disruptive change, a radical transformation. John F. Kennedy said, "Man on the Moon." The US was stirred as a nation. Lal Bhadur Shastri said, "Jai Jawan-Jai Kisan." India was stirred as a nation. Bill Gates dreamt "Desktop in every home." It shook the business. Dhirubhai Ambani said, "Phone call at the cost of a post-card." There are 800 million mobiles in India today. We need more thought leaders in our industry, in our society, in our nation and, at this time, in our history, more than ever before, especially since the doubts are lingering in recent times as to whether India can do it. It is these thought leaders alone, who can bring back that much needed spirit—yes, we can!

Raghav Bahl
Photo courtesy of Raghav Bahl

131

Kumar Mangalam Birla
Photo courtesy of Kumar Mangalam Birla

Mr Kumar Mangalam Birla receiving NASSCOM's "Global Business Leader Award 2012" from the Hon'ble Minister of Home Affairs, Mr P. Chidambaram.

Photo courtesy of Kumar Mangalam Birla

Tarun Das
Photo courtesy of Tarun Das

Tarun Das with late Prime Minister Rajiv Gandhi at the 9th IETF Fair in 1991 at Pragati Maidan, New Delhi.

Photo courtesy of Tarun Das

Adi Godrej
Photo courtesy of Adi Godrej

Chanda Kochchar

Photo courtesy of Chanda Kochchar

R. A. Mashelkar
Photo courtesy of R. A. Mashelkar

"Investment in Science is investment in India's future," explains Dr Mashelkar to the Prime Minister during the S. S. Bhatnagar Award (2005) function.

Photo courtesy of Pallava Bagla

N. R. Narayana Murthy

Photo courtesy of N. R. Narayana Murthy

Mr N. R. Narayana Murthy with the Infosys top management at the Nasdaq Remote
Opening function on the eve of Infosys' Silver Jubilee Celebrations, Mysore, July 31, 2006.

Photo courtesy of N. R. Narayana Murthy

Deepak Parekh
Photo courtesy of Deepak Parekh

Receiving the Padma Bhushan award in 2006.

Photo courtesy of Deepak Parekh

M. V. Subbiah
Photo courtesy of M. V. Subbiah

The Board Members of EID Parry, at Mr Subbiah's retirement from the Board in February 2004.

Photo courtesy of M. V. Subbiah

Profiles of the Leaders

Raghav Bahl

Raghav Bahl founded the TV18 group (now called the Network18 group) and also serves as the Managing Director of Network18, the parent company of our majority shareholder. Mr Bahl has over 25 years' experience in television and journalism. He won the Sanskriti Award for Journalism in 1994. He was selected by Ernst & Young as Entrepreneur of the Year in 2007. Mr Bahl has been awarded the AIMA Award for the Media Person of the Year in 2011, and Business Marketing Association (BMA) recognized him as the Entrepreneur of the Year in 2011. Mr Bahl has been instrumental in crafting joint ventures with companies like CNBC for CNBC TV18 and CNBC Awaaz, Time Warner for CNN IBN, Forbes Media for Forbes India magazine, A&E Networks for History—TV18, and Viacom for Viacom18, which houses Colors,

MTV, VH1, and Nickelodeon operations in India. Mr Bahl's book *SUPERPOWER? The Amazing Race Between China's Hare And India's Tortoise* was published by Penguin Allen Lane in August 2010. He holds a bachelor's degree in economics from St Stephen's College, University of Delhi, a master's degree in business administration from the University of Delhi, and a doctor of philosophy, honoris causa, from Amity University, Uttar Pradesh.

Kumar Mangalam Birla

Kumar Mangalam Birla is the Chairman of the Aditya Birla Group. He took over as Chairman of the Group in 1995 at the age of 28 years. In the 17 years that he has been at the helm of the group, its turnover has risen from US$2 billion in 1995 to over of US$40 billion today, and operations in 8 countries then to 36 countries today.

Mr Birla holds several key positions on various regulatory and professional boards. He is a Director on the Central Board of Directors of the Reserve Bank of India. Earlier, he was Chairman of the Advisory Committee (Ministry of Company Affairs) and also served on the Prime Minister of India's Advisory Council on Trade and Industry.

As the Chairman of Securities and Exchange Board of India (SEBI) Committee on Corporate Governance, he authored the First Report on Corporate Governance titled "Report of the Kumar Mangalam Birla Committee on Corporate Governance." He is also on the National Council of CII, the Apex Advisory Council of ASSOCHAM, and the Advisory Council for the Centre for Corporate Governance.

Among other accolades received by Mr Birla feature Global Business Leader Award (NASSCOM), the JRD Tata Corporate Leadership Award (AIMA), Business Leader (*The Economic Times*), Business Man of the Year Award (*Business Standard*), Business Leader of the Year Award (Lakshmipat Singhania IIM-Lucknow National Leadership Awards), Young Global Leaders (World Economic Forum), Young Super Performer in the CEO Category (*Business Today*), Entrepreneur of the Year (Forbes India Leadership Awards), and National Business Icon Award (Indore Management Association).

Mr Birla is the Chancellor of the Birla Institute of Technology & Science (BITS Pilani, Goa, Hyderabad, and Dubai) and a Director of the G. D. Birla Medical Research and Education Foundation.

A chartered accountant, Mr Birla earned an MBA from the London Business School, where he is also an Honorary Fellow and sits on the Asia Regional Advisory Board. Benaras Hindu University, G. D. Pant University of Agriculture & Technology, SRM University, and Visvesvaraya Technological University have conferred honorary doctoral degrees on Mr Birla.

Tarun Das

Tarun Das has dedicated his professional career to the development and promotion of Indian industry. Starting in November 1963 with the predecessor body of CII, he was the Director General and Chief

Executive of CII from April 1967 to May 2004 and the Chief Mentor from June 2004 to October 2009. His leadership of the organization over three decades has led to achievements in strengthening business and strategic ties between India and the world.

He is a member of several Government of India bodies under the aegis of Ministry of Finance, Planning Commission, Ministry of Human Resources Development, Ministry of External Affairs, and Ministry of Culture. He is also a member of Kerala State Planning Board, Government of Kerala. He is associated with several Indian and international institutions and bodies. These include Council on Energy Environment and Water (CEEW), World Wildlife Fund – India (WWF), Public Interest Foundation (PIF), Sasakawa India Leprosy Foundation (SILF), Indian Council for Research on International Economic Relations (ICRIER), Singapore, India Partnership Foundation (SIPF), Aspen Institute, India and US, and the East-West Center.

Adi Godrej

Adi Godrej is the Chairman of the Godrej Group, a 115-year-old family conglomerate. He is an industrialist and a philanthropist.

He joined the group after completing his Bachelors and Masters degrees in Management from the Sloan School of Management at Massachusetts Institute of Technology (USA). Throughout his career, he has systemized management structures and brought about several process improvements in the group which helped the group to meet the challenges of globalization and rise to new heights.

Mr Godrej has been president of several Indian trade and industry bodies and associations. He holds the coveted post of President of CII (2012–2013).

He is the Chairman of the Board of the Indian School of Business (Hyderabad). He has been a member of the Dean's Advisory Council of the MIT Sloan School of Management, Chairman of the Board of Governors of Narsee Monjee Institute of Management Studies, and a member of the Wharton Asian Executive Board.

Mr Godrej is a recipient of several awards and recognitions including the Rajiv Gandhi Award 2002, the Entrepreneur of the Year (Asia Pacific Entrepreneurship Awards 2010), Best Businessman of the Year (GQ Men of the Year Awards 2010), Life Time Achievement Award 2010 (Chemexil), JRD Tata Corporate Leadership Award 2010 (AIMA), Management Man of the Year Award 2010–2011 (BMA), and Qimpro Platinum Standard Award 2011 for Business.

Chanda Kochhar

Chanda Kochhar is the Managing Director and CEO of ICICI Bank Limited. She began her career with ICICI as a management trainee in 1984 and has risen through the ranks by handling multidimensional assignments and heading all the major functions in the bank at various points in time.

She is widely recognized for her role in shaping the retail banking sector in India and for her leadership of the ICICI Group.

She took on the challenge of building the nascent retail business, with strong focus on technology, innovation, process reengineering, and expansion of distribution and scale. She led the bank's corporate and international banking businesses during a period of heightened activity and global expansion by Indian companies. She was the Joint Managing Director and Chief Financial Officer during a critical period of rapid change in the global financial landscape. She was awarded the Padma Bhushan, one of India's highest civilian honors, in 2011.

R. A. Mashelkar

Dr R. A. Mashelkar, National Research Professor, is presently also the President of Global Research Alliance, a network of publicly funded R&D institutes from Asia-Pacific, Europe, and USA with over 60,000 scientists. Dr Mashelkar served as the Director General of Council of Scientific and Industrial Research (CSIR), with 40 laboratories and about 20,000 employees for over 11 years. He was also the President of Indian National Science Academy.

Dr Mashelkar is on the Board of Directors of several reputed companies such as Reliance Industries Ltd., Tata Motors Ltd., Hindustan Unilever Ltd., Thermax Ltd., Piramal Enterprises Ltd., KPIT Cummins Infosystems Ltd., etc. Deeply connected with the innovation movement in India, Dr Mashelkar is currently the Chairman of India's National Innovation Foundation, Reliance Innovation Council, Thermax Innovation Council, KPIT Cummins Innovation Council, and Marico Innovation Foundation.

Dr Mashelkar is only the third Indian engineer in the 20th century to have been elected (in 1998) as a Fellow of Royal Society (FRS), London. He was elected Foreign Associate of National Academy of Science (USA) in 2005, Associate Foreign Member, American Academy of Arts & Sciences (2011), Foreign Fellow of US National Academy of Engineering (2003), and Fellow of Royal Academy of Engineering, UK (1996). Thirty universities have honored him with honorary doctorates, which include Universities of London, Salford, Pretoria, Wisconsin, and Delhi.

In August 1997, *Business India* named Dr Mashelkar as being among the 50 pathbreakers in post-Independent India. On November 16, 2005, he received the *BusinessWeek* (USA) award of "Stars of Asia" at the hands of George Bush (Sr.), the former president of USA. He was the first Asian scientist to receive it.

In post-liberalization India, Dr Mashelkar has played a critical role in shaping India's science and technology policies. He was a member of the Scientific Advisory Council to the Prime Minister of India in the past three decades. The President of India honored Dr Mashelkar with the Padma Shri in 1991 and with the Padma Bhushan in 2000.

N. R. Narayana Murthy

N. R. Narayana Murthy is the Founder of Infosys Limited, a global software consulting company headquartered in Bangalore, India. He founded Infosys in 1981, served as the CEO during 1981–2002, and as the Chairman and Chief Mentor during 1981–2011.

Under his leadership, Infosys was listed on NASDAQ in 1999. He is currently the Chairman Emeritus of Infosys.

Mr Murthy articulated, designed, and implemented the Global Delivery Model, has led key corporate governance initiatives in India, and is an IT advisor to several Asian countries.

He has served on the boards of several leading universities, institutes, and organizations and is currently on the boards of HSBC, Ford Foundation, Rhodes Trust, Indian School of Business, and the UN Foundation.

Mr Murthy was listed as one among the "12 Greatest Entrepreneurs of Our Time" by the *Fortune* magazine in 2012. He is the recipient of several prestigious awards including the Padma Vibhushan by the Government of India, the Légion d'honneur by the Government of France, and the Commander of the Most Excellent Order of the British Empire (CBE) by the Government of UK. He is the first Indian winner of Ernst and Young's World Entrepreneur of the Year award and the Max Schmidheiny Liberty Prize. He has appeared in the rankings of businessmen and innovators published by *BusinessWeek*, *Time*, CNN, *Fortune*, *India Today*, *Business Standard*, *Forbes*, and the *Financial Times*.

Deepak Parekh

Deepak Parekh, Chairman, HDFC spearheads India's leading Financial Services conglomerate with presence in banking, asset management, life insurance, general insurance, real estate venture fund, and education loans.

He is the Non-Executive Chairman of Glaxo Smithkline Pharmaceuticals, IDFC, and Siemens India. He is also on the boards of Mahindra & Mahindra, Indian Hotels and international board of DP World, UAE. In addition, he is also on the advisory boards of several Indian corporations and MNCs.

He has been dubbed as the unofficial crisis consultant of the Government of India and is a member of various high-powered advisory committees and task forces.

Some of his significant recognitions are: received the Padma Bhushan in 2006; received the "Knight in the Order of the Legion of Honour," one of the highest distinction by the French Republic, in 2010; was the first international recipient of the ICAEW Outstanding Achievement Award—2010.

M. V. Subbiah

M. V. Subbiah is a third-generation member of the Murugappa family. He is the former chairman of Murugappa Group and retired in January 2004 after working for 43 years in the family business. He played an important role in transforming a number of group companies such as Carborundum Universal in the 1960s, T. I. Cycles in the 1970s, and EID Parry in the 1980s.

Currently he is the Managing Trustee of the Murugappa family foundation, the AMM Foundation, and the Chairman of a newly formed public–private corporation called the National Skill Development Corporation (NSDC), which is mandated to skill 150 million youths in India by 2022.

In the past, Mr Subbiah has been associated with number of organizations such as Association of Indian Engineering Industries, the predecessor of Confederation of Indian Industry (CII); Family Business Network International; Madras Crafts Foundation (DakshinaChitra); WORTH Trust (Workshop of the Rehabilitation of the Handicapped); and India Foundation for the Arts.

Mr Subbiah has been a recipient of the JRD Tata Corporate Leadership Award in 2002 and the National HRD Award in 1988. The Murugappa family is a recipient of the Distinguished Family Business Award from IMD Lausanne in 2001. Birmingham University (UK) recognized his contribution to business by awarding him an honorary doctorate in 2011. He was also conferred with the prestigious Padma Bhushan by the President of India in 2012 for his contribution to trade and commerce.